Virginia's Legendary
SANTA TRAINS

• DONNA STROTHER DEEKENS & DOUG RIDDELL •

Published by The History Press
Charleston, SC 29403
www.historypress.net

Back cover, top: Santa climbs aboard the observation car of an N&W overnight streamliner en route back to the North Pole, 1950. *Courtesy Norfolk Southern Corp*; *top left*: A local newspaper ad lists the dates and times of the Richmond Miller & Rhoads Santa Trains, indicating how quickly their popularity had spread. *Lewis Parks Private Collection*; *bottom left*: The company photographer captured this image of an admiring child giving Santa her wish list on board a Norfolk & Western Railway passenger train in December 1957. *Courtesy Norfolk Southern Corp.*

First published 2013

Manufactured in the United States

ISBN 978.1.62619.140.2

Library of Congress CIP data applied for.

To my wonderful husband, Bill, whose endearing and enduring memories of the Fifth and Grace Streets train display window from his boyhood in the 1950s and 1960s at Miller & Rhoads in downtown Richmond at Christmas and whose very special love for and devotion to "his Snow Queen" served as an inspiration to make this book possible.

—DSD

My dreams are reality because of the love and sacrifice of a remarkable woman—my wife, Sandra. In my absence from home as a working railroader, she ably raised our wonderful son, Ryan. My modest success as a writer bears the mark of her support and guidance. This book would have been impossible to write but for her patience and understanding.

—ADR

CONTENTS

ACKNOWLEDGEMENTS

We are indebted to many people for this work, both tangibly and intangibly, about Virginia's legendary Santa Trains. Among them are Ken Miller and the Roanoke Chapter, National Railway Historical Society; Beth Miller; the late Claudine Miller; J.L. Saunders; the late Charles Curley Jr.; Charles Curley III; Bob Dickinson; Bill Whitbeck; Calvin Boles; Bill Todd and the membership of the Old Dominion Chapter of the National Railway Historical Society; William E. Griffin Jr., retired RF&P/CSX executive and rail historian; Jim Musgrove; Dale Latham and the members of the RF&P RR Historical Society; Richard Beadles, retired president, RF&P RR; Mr. and Mrs. Jim Grem; George Bryson; Carol Hudgens Bryson; Sue Ferrell; the late Eugene "Gene" Luck; Bob Luck; Beth Luck; Charles Nuckols; Wes Nuckols; Dan Rowe; Fran Rowe; Tina Currie; Nancy Bumgardner; Nancy Allen Perrow; Harriet Heath; Ed Heath; Celeste Heath; Melodie Heath Warren; Lewis Parks; Lisa McDaniel Ramos; the late H. Reid, author and railroad historian; the late Milton Burke; Bertha Burke; Penn Burke; Victoria Burke; Bonnie Burke Ball; Deborah Crawford; the late William Strother; Ray McAllister and *Boomer* magazine; Cheryl Miller and Torri Strickland of WTVR CBS 6; Morgan Dean of WRIC TV8; Martha Steger; Nancy Pace Newton; the late Bob Jeffers; Gwen Jeffers Downey; Rosanne Shalf and the Ashland Museum; Mary Anna Tignor Sylvia; Suzanne Huff; Lanie Covington Turnage; Betsy Hodges; members of the Cox and Andrews families of Ashland, especially Betty Carol Stevenson and Cecile Cox; Laurie Preston and the McGraw-Page Library at Randolph-Macon College; Jan Walker and Hickory Creek Antiques; Sumpter T. Priddy

Jr.; Tom Wulf and the Ashland Main Street Association; Sarah Wright; Bill Ewald; Pat Ewald; Jim Donlan; Cathy Willis Waldrop; Kim Gillis; the Richard S. Gillis Jr./Ashland Branch Library; Dan Sherrier and the *Herald-Progress*; Walter Loftin; H.B. Bryant; Anne Bryant; the Sedley Woman's Club, especially June Hundley Dunlow and Nancy Cogsdale; Donna Neal Turner; Tommy Turner; Joan Hundley Powell; Bernadette Whitley; Lucy Minetree Wallace and the *Tidewater News*; Patricia Duck Carter; Jim Creasey; Peggy Darden Rush; Lynne Hubbard Rabil; Hubbard Peanut Company, Inc.; the Hudgins family, especially Janet Hudgins, Donna Kingery Hudgins and Carter L. Hudgins; Jack Hundley; Wesley Wills; Elizabeth Johnson; Cynthia Johnson Stone; the late Elvin Whitley; Jane March and the Zuni Historical Society; Joe Brinkley Jr.; Steve Barry and Carstens Publications, Inc.; Lindsey Nair, Belinda Harris and the *Roanoke Times*; Gail McMillan and John Jackson of Virginia Tech Special Collections; Nathan Flinchum, Dyron Knick and the Virginia Room of the Roanoke Public Library; Julia Stewart Milton; Ginger Hibbetts Sweet; the late Arthur "Chuck" Hood; the late Frances Hood; Carolyn Hood Drudge; Marilyn Hood Gunn; Robin Hood; Nancy Bendall Emerson; Ben Emerson; Joan Bendall; John Bendall Jr.; Paul Mitchell; Tim Mitchell; Mary Mitchell Amos; Ed Crews; Bobbie Kay Wash; John Whiting; Lynn Taylor; the late Charlie Wakefield; Cheryl Wakefield Hamm; Paul Pearce; John Schultheis; the late Henry Gonner; Hank Gonner; Jack West; Fred Dill; Tom Mitchell; Hank Coghill; Dorman Hartley; the late Eddie Weaver; Jody Weaver Yuhase; Ken Martin; Lee Hawkins; Graham Wilson; Charles Hladik; Gareth Quale; Bernard Baldwin; Tom Ledford; Kim Vickers; Wendy Morton; Tony Turner; Marc Goswick; Jean Howe Duke; Gail Patterson Brookings; Linda Taylor; Dale Parris; Jack Arthur; Tom Long; Lee Milstead; Tom Williams; Phillip Wenz; "Santa Ray"; Joe Pace; George Thomas Parsons III; Troy Valos and the Sargeant Memorial Collection of the Norfolk Public Library; Clyde Nordan and Olde Towne Photos of Portsmouth, Virginia; David Cartier; Ruby Atkinson; the city of Portsmouth, Virginia; the Portsmouth Museums Foundation; Gary Sease at CSX Corp; Chipp Boone of Keolis Virginia/VRE and his wife, Cindy; Chuck McIntyre; Michael Lisicky; Annabel Woodriff Newton; Edythe Gill; Connie Nimmo; Marie Cotten; the late Carlton McKenney; Beth McKenney; Gale Spriggs; Don Spriggs; Earlene Bayliss; Pat Cully; Bill Schafer, retired vice-president, Norfolk Southern Corp; Jennifer McDaid and Norfolk Southern Corp.; the Crewe Railroad Museum; the Library of Virginia; Lora Spiller and Dominion Power; Bill Martin, Meg Hughes, Kelly Kerney and the Valentine Richmond History Center; Cold Harbor Antiques;

Coalfield Station Antiques; Old Chickahominy House, Williamsburg, Virginia; Forest Hill Antiques; Sixty West Antique Mall; de Rochonnet Delights Chocolatier; Vaughan Gary; Rick Smith; Dottie Mears; Tom Mears; Debby Robertson; Woody Robertson; Dr. Robert Quarles; Dr. Joe Niamtu; Joan Barns; Bill Barns; Ann James; Earl Roth; Wayne Peters; Pam Spicer Anderson; Sally Wooldridge Canar; Beverly Hargrove Edwards; Dennis Wrenn; Judy Wrenn; June Lacy; Leeanne Ladin; J. Banks Smither; Julia Turner; John Strother; Judith Strother Jones; Ron Jones; Mike Jones; Amy Jones; Brent Deekens; Greg Deekens; Josh Yeager; Kathy Deekens; Andy Deekens; Anne Deekens; Earle Dunford; and Ryan and Hope Riddell. Extra thanks to our patient and supportive spouses, Bill Deekens and Sandy Riddell.

Any errors are the sole responsibility of the authors and not those who offered their assistance.

INTRODUCTION

Into Town on a Rail

It made no difference to me that the temperature was below freezing or that my feet were cold. It did annoy me, however, that the warm air from my nose, which was pressed up against the Fifth and Grace Streets display window of Richmond's downtown Miller & Rhoads department store, fogged up the glass each time I exhaled. Unfortunately, this occluded my view of the wondrous, twinkling diorama of the commonwealth of Virginia, spotlighting each of the store's statewide branch locations. Of more importance to me were the model trains that hurtled into and out of tunnels, across bridges and along the iron network of tracks that connected large cities and small towns. For an alternative view, I'd work my way around the corner to the Fifth Street window, snickering at the other boys and girls, whose noses and hands were likewise flattened as they peered into the window. How strange they looked. It never once occurred to me that I probably appeared just as malformed to them as they did to me. But who cared? We were filled with thoughts of Christmas.

An HO scale Chesapeake & Ohio Railroad freight train smoothly crossed the long, high viaduct that resembled the one skirting the north bank of the James River, just a few blocks away, allowing mile-long strings of loaded black coal hoppers to rumble past the burgeoning skyline of Virginia's capital city en route to the port of Hampton Roads. On that same long viaduct, in the afternoons, my grandmother and I would stand on the brow of Richmond's Chimborazo Park, near our Church Hill home, to wave at the C&O's George Washington passenger train, slowing for its arrival at

Santa makes his way down the aisle of an RF&P/Miller & Rhoads Santa Train car, 1963. *William E. Griffin Private Collection.*

Richmond's venerable Main Street station. Excitedly, I could spot my grandfather, the conductor, leaning out the top half of the rear car's Dutch door, returning our waves.

In the store window, on a parallel track, was a purple and silver Atlantic Coast Line diesel with aluminum coaches. It was complete with silhouettes of travelers in each window fleeing the wintry Northeast, headed for the balmy sands of Miami Beach in pre–Disney World Florida.

I purposely overlooked the fact that the streamlined O scale Lionel Santa Fe Super Chief, speeding along a track occupying the bottom of the window, never actually wandered east of Chicago. I wanted one like it, just the same. Joe Wade, the Miller & Rhoads shoe department buyer and a member of our church, had not only a Super Chief but also a Lionel collection. His treasures included a huffing, chuffing New York Central Niagara steam locomotive, busily hauling freight cars and trailed by a little red caboose. Small of stature, he held up his suit trousers with a pair of his signature suspenders. With feet so small that he had to special order men's size-five shoes on his trips to the merchandise market in New York City annually, Joe Wade was nonetheless a "big kid." Each year, the entirety of the front room of his T Street home, in the working-class Fairmount section of Church Hill, was cleared of furniture in order to make way for an enormous, star-topped

Miller & Rhoads' downtown Richmond Fifth and Grace Streets window display of Virginia cities. *Milton Burke Private Collection.*

Christmas fir, festooned with everything imaginable. Laid meticulously beneath its branches was a seemingly endless wonderland in miniature—trees, fences, brightly lit cottages and oscillating airport beacons. Milk cans were loaded into refrigerated boxcars as wooden poles were rolled onto flat cars. Each scene was connected, as if by magic, with shiny nickel-silver Lionel tracks.

On the Sunday night before Christmas, I would anxiously squirm in the pew in the balcony during our church's Christmas pageant, knowing that at its conclusion, we'd pile into our old Plymouth or walk the short three blocks to the Wade home. There, while the choir members dissected the pageant's musical accompaniment, critiquing the evening's high points and flat notes over cups of cocoa and (nonalcoholic, thank you) eggnog, Joe and I would grab the twin handles of the big black Lionel dual-control transformer to race the Super Chief and the big Niagara around the layout. The contest continued until one or both derailed or until my parents could gather the energy to pry their eldest son away from the controls. Not even the box containing pieces of sticky hard candy we'd received in Sunday school earlier in the day could quiet me as I screamed, kicked and cried, as if I was to be sent off to some horrid place where there were no trains. After all, as a child (and later, as an adult), mine was a world of trains.

I was no less willing to leave my hard-earned vantage point in front of the display window at that popular M&R corner when my sisters, Lynette and Marcia, summoned me inside for the elevator ride up to the store's renowned Tea Room. With our mom, we would anxiously fidget in line for an hour to dine with Santa. Oh, this was no ordinary Santa Claus, as anyone within a hundred-mile radius of Richmond would steadfastly attest. This was the real Santa. It wasn't necessary for the Post Office Department—an official agency of the United States government—to declare him to be the one and only Santa Claus, à la the classic Christmas film *Miracle on 34th Street* (which starred Roanoke, Virginia native John Payne).[1] No, with his white rabbit fur–trimmed red velvet suit, white gloves, polished Italian black leather boots and gracefully bearded face—sculpted and colored by Hollywood makeup icon Max Factor—the Miller & Rhoads Santa was, without a doubt, "the real McCoy."[2] His loyal following was composed of parents and their children by the thousands, from as far away as Tidewater and Southwest Virginia, the Carolinas and the Washington suburbs, who traveled to Richmond by car, bus and train.

Once we finally were seated to dine in the Tea Room, our meal with Santa, the Snow Queen and Mischievous Little Elf was properly topped off with a slice of Rudolph Cake. It was washed down with a big glass of ice-cold milk, perfectly timed to coincide with a comic keyboard spiral by celebrated theater organist Eddie Weaver on the Tea Room's Hammond. Once the last drop disappeared, so did the jolly ol' elf, reappearing moments later in Santaland, on the Fifth Floor. There, after checking in with the radiantly smiling Snow Queen, kids from 1 to 101 could confide their hearts' desire for Christmas morning to Santa and have their pictures taken seated on his lap. Somehow, this Santa magically greeted each and every child by name, so he most certainly knew who had been bad or good.

And for many years, from 1957 to 1971, this Santa arrived in Richmond in style, at Broad Street Station, aboard a twenty-coach Richmond, Fredericksburg & Potomac Railroad train. Early on the Saturday mornings prior to Christmas, a sold-out crowd of around 1,500 adults and children filled the cavernous concourse of the 1919 John Russell Pope transportation cathedral, awaiting the announcement to board the Miller & Rhoads Santa Special.

At the appointed moment, the terminal's gateman opened the doors and then stood back as he unleashed a flood of jubilant youngsters, who cascaded down the stairs and flooded the platform. Towering beside that platform, the Santa Special awaited them.

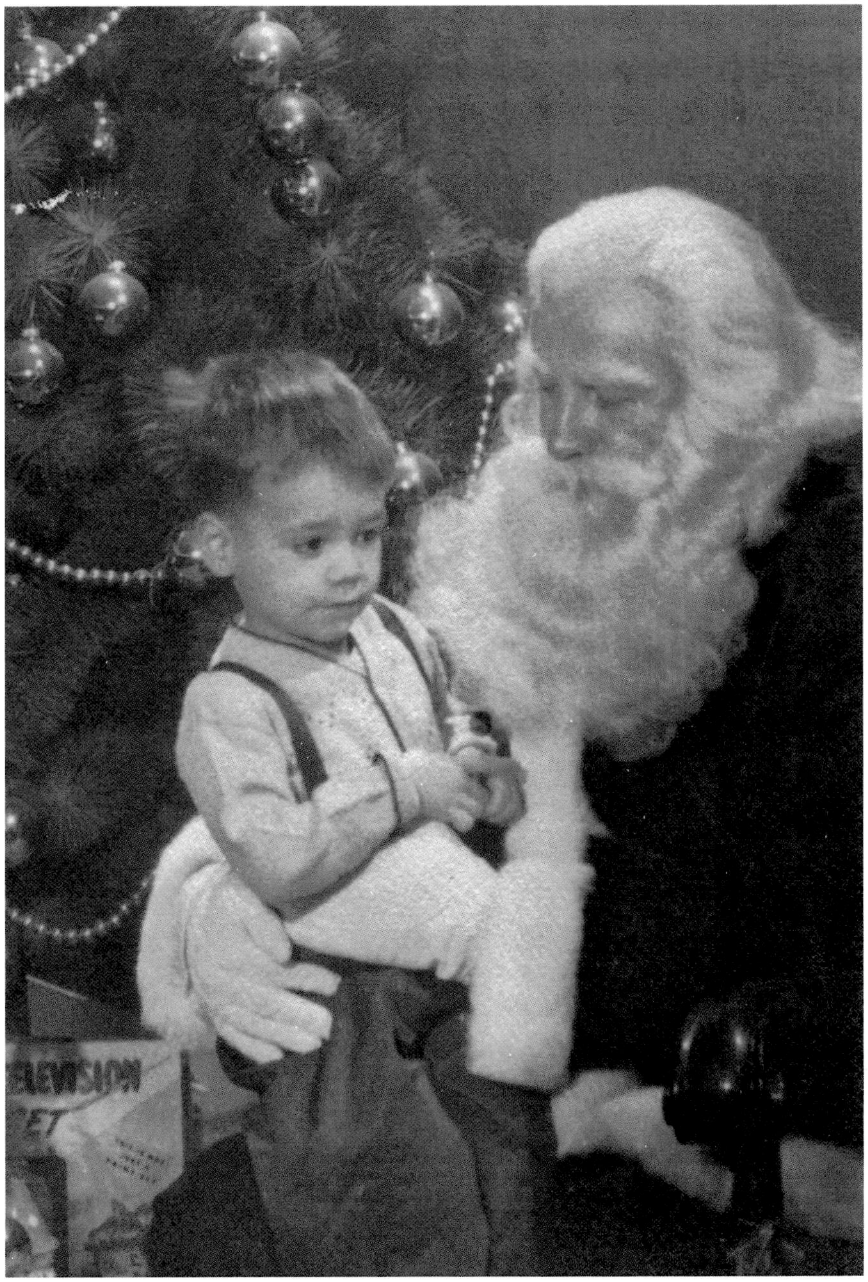

Doug Riddell, age three, visits with the "Real Santa" at Miller & Rhoads in Richmond, 1952. *Doug Riddell Private Collection.*

Santa Train passengers prepare to board the Richmond to Ashland Christmas trip, 1959. *William E. Griffin Private Collection.*

Clamoring up the train's steps, ecstatic children poured into the aisles of each car, quickly finding seats, jumping on the cushions, screaming to the tops of their voices and waving to loved ones standing outside who waved back. With two toots from the horn of the lead diesel locomotive, the train began to move north—not to the North Pole (although the children were told they were going to that magical land), but to the town of Ashland, about eighteen miles (fifteen minutes) away, where Santa and his Snow Queen awaited them. It was explained to the curious that Rudolph and the other reindeer were resting at a secret location in order to be ready for Santa's big night. The mission had begun: to pick up Santa Claus and bring him to Richmond.

As if the little ones needed further enticement, clowns roamed the train once it left the station and began to pick up speed as it passed through the railroad's freight yards. The grays of the city gave way to the greens of the suburbs, finally yielding to the open fields of the countryside. No sooner had the Santa Special reached its cruising speed than it gently began to slow down for Ashland, where the tracks bisected the main thoroughfare (appropriately named Railroad Street), and the twenty blue, gray and gold railroad cars were reflected in the windows of the antebellum mansions that lined both sides of the right of way. Slower and slower it moved until it stopped at Ashland's quaint brick depot, where Kris Kringle stood waiting with his stunningly beautiful young Snow Queen at his side.

Farther north the train rambled, taking the siding (an adjacent track) at Doswell or Milford, where the locomotives were detached and run around to the opposite end of the Special so that the train, full of joyous celebrants, would head south, arriving at Broad Street Station—an arrival that seemed to be much too soon.

It's hard to put into words the thrill I had as a child, reaching out to touch Santa, to tell him that I wanted a Lionel Super Chief under our tree when my siblings and I awoke on Christmas morning. "That's a mighty tall order. Have you been real good?" I remember him asking me with a look that included furrowed eyebrows but also the hint of a smile.

"Yes sir, Santa. You know I've been good," I responded without hesitation, crossing my fingers and hoping he took in account that young boys my age detested brussels sprouts and despised liver and onions. And I refused to eat them, even when my mother made me sit at the table until long after everyone else had left.

No, Santa never did bring me that Lionel Super Chief. And I don't think it had anything at all to do with brussels sprouts or liver and onions. Also, I don't believe it had anything to do with those report cards from teachers who summarized my early school years, citing my propensity for imagination or daydreaming. It had an awful lot more to do with a father, mother and four small children who struggled to put brussels sprouts, liver and onions or anything else on the table, clothes on our backs and a roof over our heads. My folks—God rest their sainted souls—saw to it that while we didn't have everything, we did the most with everything we did have. And we had what counted most: their love, their guidance and the benefit of their wisdom and faith.

At age sixty-three, I still believe in Santa Claus, even after a playmate broke my heart and shattered my world. He opened the coat closet in his living room one wintry morning before Christmas and showed me the Chatty Cathy doll his younger sister was going to get "from Santa." (My mother, while full of Christian charity, never forgave my little friend.) But, you see, some years ago, after Joe Wade passed away at a young age ninety-six, I inherited his Santa Fe Super Chief. It's a bit battered and scratched but seasoned. A year or so before Joe's last Christmas, I'd taken my son, Ryan (now an Amtrak locomotive engineer, like his father), to Joe's home in the suburbs, where the three of us thrilled ourselves by racing it and the big Lionel Niagara around his holiday wonder world. To this day, it is one of my

Norfolk & Western employee magazine cover, December 1962. *Courtesy Norfolk Southern Corp.*

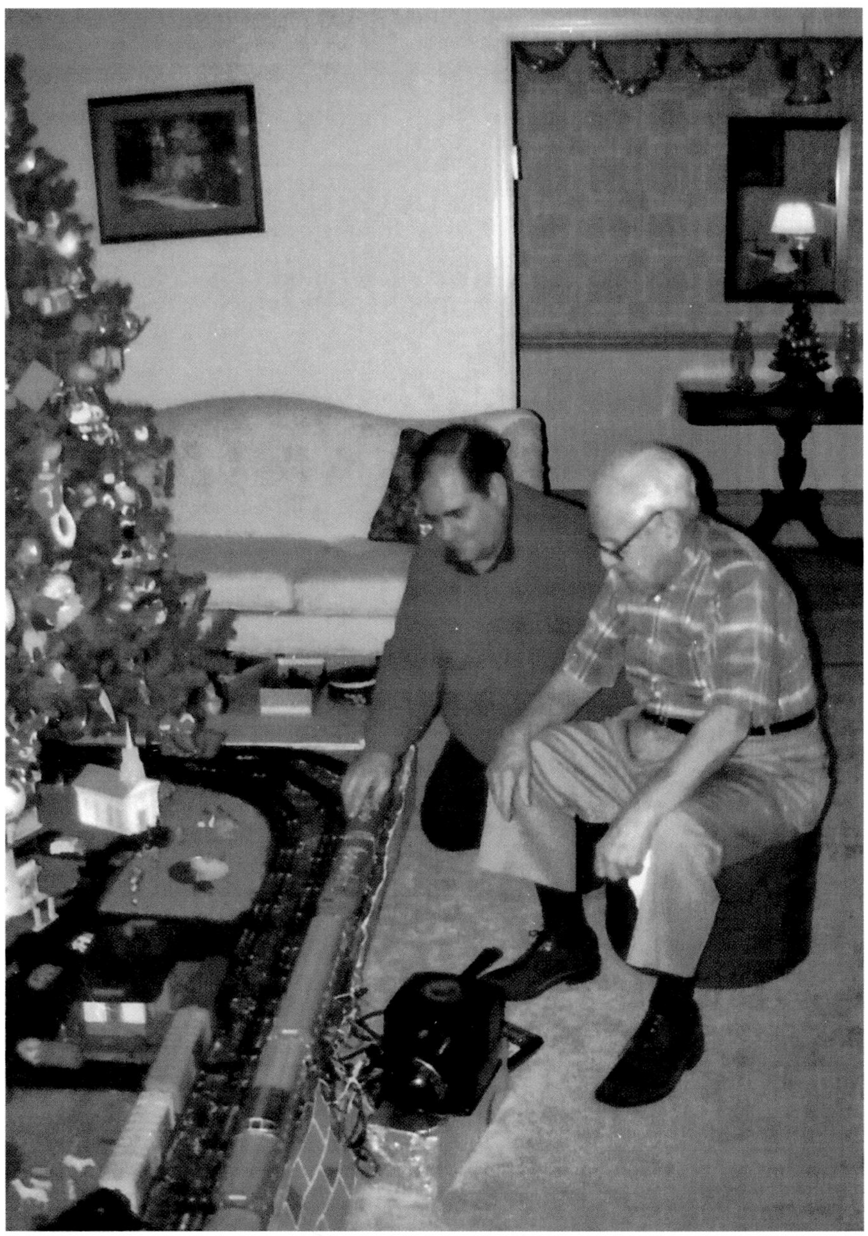

Retired Miller & Rhoads shoe buyer Joe Wade (right) at home with his Lionel trains and Doug Riddell (left), 1996. *Doug Riddell Private Collection.*

most treasured possessions, and it always will be, until it becomes my son's. I hope it will be passed on to a grandchild one day.

Along with those silver and red Santa Fe diesels and shiny aluminum cars, memories rush back of the Fifth and Grace Streets Miller & Rhoads window, Richmond's "Real" Santa, his Snow Queen, Eddie Weaver and the Tea Room and the excitement of arriving on the Santa Train in Ashland, Virginia. It is in this iconic town that I now happily reside in retirement, following a career as a locomotive engineer, at the throttle of the trains that burnish those very same rails I rode as a child.

When former Miller & Rhoads longtime Snow Queen Donna Strother Deekens asked me if I'd consider coauthoring a book with her about the wonderful Santa Trains that brought Christmas joy to generations of Virginians, I couldn't turn her down. After all, I had her to help me, along with Santa and the recollections of thousands of one-time youngsters who now have year-round "snow atop their own roofs." Those reminiscences are as bright as a fireplace hearth at Christmas, keeping the memories as warm as if it were yesterday.

All aboard!

CHAPTER 1

A STROKE OF GOOD LUCK

It was 1955. World War II had been over for ten years. Dwight David Eisenhower, the general who had commanded the forces of the victorious Allies, now served his country again, but as president, and led a nation with an unbridled thirst to pursue peace and prosperity. Even the so-called police action in Korea had not managed to deter Americans from the manifest destiny they envisioned.

Rosie the Riveter had surrendered her place on the war-effort assembly line to returning servicemen. By the thousands, they had come home, married and started families. Empowered by the GI Bill, they reentered high schools to obtain their diplomas or enrolled in colleges to pursue degrees. Swords were being turned into plow shears, the nation's economic engine had a full head of steam and the train of prosperity was pulling out of the station.

In Virginia, thousands of acres of farms and woodland were cleared and quickly began sprouting a new crop of homes, schools, industries and businesses at a pace barely able to keep up with demand. Heretofore-rationed products, or those that had not been available at all during the war, began magically appearing.

Downtown department stores followed their customer base out of town—at first, tepidly renting space in the suburban shopping center while even enlarging and maintaining their city-center flagship locations. The shopping center was a new phenomenon that allowed customers to drive a short distance from their homes, park their new automobiles and walk directly into the front entrance of department store branch locations or specialty

Take the "if" out of Gift
ELECTRICALLY!
WATCH FAMILY FACES looking in an electric appliance window. You'll see why this is the place to pick gifts with no "if" about them being wanted!
THERE'S A GLEAM IN DAD'S EYE as he focuses on that Electric Slide Projector. Just what he needs to make his color photos really come alive.
MOM HAS A LONGING LOOK as she thinks of all the arm-wearying chores that Electric Mixer would do for her . . . from juicing oranges to beating cakes.
SIS HAS HER MIND ON that portable Electric Record Player. She knows what its new type hi-fi tone could do for some of her latest sizzling platters!
AND SON IS TAKING IN every realistic detail of that toy Electric Train, with remote-control signals and switches.

TODAY'S SANTA ENTERS HERE!
GIVE YOUR HOME an electric entrance to fit today's electric gifts . . . and tomorrow's! Get a three-wire link with the power line, plus at least a 100-amp fuse panel, at today's new low cost for single family homes. Your electrical contractor will gladly give you an estimate on modern HOUSEPOWER, YOUR POWER TO LIVE BETTER ELECTRICALLY!

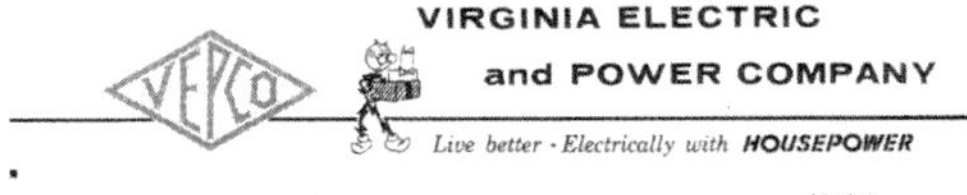

VEPCO
VIRGINIA ELECTRIC
and POWER COMPANY
Live better · Electrically with HOUSEPOWER
12·6·2

A family of the 1950s window shops at Christmas in this Virginia Electric and Power Company advertisement, 1956. *With permission of Dominion Power, courtesy Library of Virginia.*

merchandisers. They didn't have to consult a schedule, stand on a corner in the pouring rain, fight downtown traffic, feed meters, risk being towed or calculate the cost of leaving the family station wagon in a parking deck. Buying anything became quick, easy and convenient, just like drive-in restaurants, supermarkets or TV dinners.

In the Richmond area, fixed trolley lines that did not extend out into the new bedroom communities of Henrico and Chesterfield Counties had already become obsolete. Rubber-tired buses, powered by gasoline or diesel fuel, could roam wherever their services were needed. Overhead electric wires, now deemed unsightly and archaic by forward-thinking Richmonders, didn't limit a bus. In a city known to be the home of the first practical electric streetcar (May 4, 1888), it was indeed a solemn day in 1949 when the last trolleys on the Highland Park line made their final run. Sadly, they were summarily hauled to a vacant lot near Church Hill and burned to separate salvageable metal from their wooden bodies.[3]

But industrial progress beckoned all who met the postwar challenges, as a new hope and vitality spread nationwide. Virginians looked on these years as promising a new beginning, with great dreams of success, stability and happiness.

Eugene Luck was well acquainted with success. According to his son Bob, Gene Luck was a man who had never sold refrigerators to Eskimos simply because he had never been to Alaska. Had the elder Luck traveled to the Klondike, there no doubt would have been a proliferation of whatever brand he was hawking. He was just that good, that sincere and that likeable.

The son of a railroad clerk, Eugene Bernard Luck was born in Selma, Alabama, in 1905. It was said that he had the disarming smile and decorum of the consummate southern gentleman, while at the same time possessing the determination of General Sherman marching from Atlanta to the sea. When he was a small child, the Luck family moved to Richmond, Virginia.[4]

In 1955, Gene Luck was ready for a career change. Four years prior, he'd applied for a position as a stenographer at the Wortendyke Paper Company, a supplier of bags used in grocery stores, at the foot of Thirteenth Street in downtown Richmond. He immediately rose through the ranks to become the company's top salesman and later was named vice-president. Nor did it take long for him to notice that the name Union Bag Company continuously surfaced in his sales calls. In Luck's way of thinking, there was opportunity here, so it came as no surprise to anyone that he engineered the sale of Wortendyke to Union Bag.

While most people would have been content to accept the reward for the organization and implementation of such a successful and lucrative business deal, Luck was not satisfied. Union Bag was a much larger and diverse company. He'd essentially be starting out again at the bottom and working his way up, so he decided to move on to seek out other opportunities.

W. Thomas Rice was also poised on the launching pad of a career that would later catapult him to unequalled heights as a major force in the history of the American rail industry. A Virginian and a VMI graduate, he had already been a military officer primarily responsible for setting into motion plans to rebuild the devastated railroad infrastructure of post–World War II Japan. Rice had also risen through the ranks of the Richmond, Fredericksburg & Potomac Railroad (RF&P). In 1955, he was the railway's president when he met Gene Luck.

Unlike the trucking industry, which viewed President Eisenhower's proposed Interstate Highway System with great enthusiasm, Rice faced the naked reality that, supplied with a government-funded, limited-access, coast-to-coast system of highways, the railroad industry's already diminishing share of the heavily regulated freight tonnage was about to take another hit.

With or without a labyrinth of concrete thruways, private automobile ownership and motor coach operators had siphoned off enough coach-class passenger traffic that most railroads' balance sheets were hemorrhaging red ink. As if that were not discouragement enough, the airlines were already gnawing away at the high-dollar ticket revenue brought in by business travelers whose companies footed the bill for first-class and Pullman sleeping car accommodations.

Tom Rice listened intently as Gene Luck reasoned that if properly advertised and promoted, good passenger service could result in increased freight revenues. Indeed, good public relations and better marketing of passenger service would help stem the direct losses the railroad currently was suffering. Seeing the RF&P through the windows of one of their coaches or sleeping cars amounted to a virtual showcase for the railroad's freight traffic development department.

"I know you want freight business, but with better passenger relations, you can get better freight business!" Bob Luck remembers his father's advice.[5] Giving people a reason to ride their trains (as opposed to simply hoping that travelers would perhaps stumble into Broad Street Station instead of the airport, the bus station or driving) was sure to bring the RF&P more riders.

While Rice was intrigued by the idea, he wasn't entirely sold on this inviting theory, so Gene Luck rolled the dice. He persuaded Tom Rice to give him six months to show a marked improvement in passenger service of the RF&P. At that time, rather than have the boss fire him if he was not happy with the results, Luck would resign. Whether the legendary railroad executive W. Thomas Rice knew it or not, the Eskimos had just bought a trainload of refrigerators.

CHAPTER 2

"THE MILLER & RHOADS OF ASHLAND"

For ten-year-old Jerry Maxey, Labor Day weekend meant his annual pilgrimage to Cox department store in Ashland, Virginia, to be fitted for his new pair of Buster Brown oxfords, underwear, socks, blue jeans and plaid shirts—his entire wardrobe for the upcoming school year.

"Don't go scuff'n 'em up. They're all you're gonna get 'til spring, when you'll get a new pair of tennis shoes," urged his father, a train dispatcher for the Richmond, Fredericksburg & Potomac Railroad. Its tracks passed directly in front of their Taylorsville home, and if passenger trains had stopped there, it would have been an easy commute. It was only five miles by rail to Ashland, as the crow flies. It took considerably longer by automobile, unfortunately, because to do so meant sharing parallel U.S. Route 1 with thousands of cars and trucks that crawled along the nation's overburdened main north–south transportation corridor, around the clock, all year long.[6]

The closer one came to Ashland, the more service stations, tourists' courts and mom-and-pop restaurants crowded the roadway, their blinking neon signs competing for attention, beckoning travelers to pull over for a tasty home-cooked meal, a good night's rest or a fill-up with twenty-cents-per-gallon motor fuel. President Eisenhower had just announced a program of limited access super highways that would speed motorists between cities. What changes Ike's Interstate Highway System would bring were anyone's guess, but for the foreseeable future, the well-worn, four-lane blacktop reigned supreme, and the small-town businesses, whose lifeblood was the commerce it brought in, were temporarily safe.

A 1913 postcard depicting the D.B. Cox department store in Ashland, Virginia's business district. *Courtesy Ashland Museum.*

For Jacqueline Andrews; her husband, Joseph; and their business partner, Fairfax Davis, the eighteen miles of U.S. 1 between Ashland and Richmond also afforded some degree of security—a buffer that served to forestall the wave of post–World War II urban sprawl north from Virginia's state capital. Cox department store was opened shortly after the Civil War, in 1867, by Mrs. Andrews's grandfather Duncan Balfour Cox.[7] It had grown from a small general store into a two-story emporium, whose address read 100 Railroad Avenue, at the crossroads of State Highway 54 and the RF&P tracks, just a stone's throw from the railroad's quaint slate-roofed depot. The stately brick buildings and columned antebellum fraternity houses of Junior Ivy League Randolph-Macon College accounted for a significant portion of trade in the second-floor men's department. The first floor was awash in fashions for the ladies of the town who tended their gardens and attended the Ashland Women's Club, as they had every second Tuesday since the war—the Civil War, that is.[8]

Cox Incorporated was thriving when three employees—the Andrewses and Davis—bought the business from the Cox family in 1955. While there were local passenger trains to Richmond that stopped in Ashland and even a little blue and white West End Transit Company bus that plied myriad country back roads—eventually delivering riders to the stores of Richmond's retail shopping core—the new owners intended to keep their business prosperous. After all, it had survived recessions, wars, fraternity pranks, the Depression and the great fire of 1893.[9]

The interior of Cox Incorporated department store in Ashland, Virginia, during the store closing sale, 1960. *Cox Family Private Collection.*

That year, flames destroyed much of Ashland's commercial district, including the frame building that housed the D.B. Cox department store. The brick and masonry that were mandated after the ruins were cleared, thanks to an enduring spirit of small-town entrepreneurial pride, resulted in the rise of not only a charming town center from Ashland's ashes but also a quaint, picturesque shopping district. While the names on some of the storefronts have changed from time to time, the attractive decades-old structures' façades remain essentially unchanged. From a practical standpoint, in a community subject to glowing embers being spewed into the air by passing steam locomotives, it simply made good sense. Quite often, until the coal-burning behemoths were ushered into railroad heaven in the early 1950s, roofs on the colorful homes that face the iron thoroughfare that bisects Ashland's tree-lined Railroad Avenue remained defenseless against occasional fires.[10] With the coming of the somewhat cleaner diesel-electric locomotives that began powering the seemingly incessant parade of trains through Ashland, it also became safer to stroll the town's sidewalks wearing white shirts or pastel-colored dresses.

In 1955, Richmond's Miller & Rhoads department store and its cross-street retail competitor, Thalhimers, were both eyeing expansion into the city's fast-growing suburbs, as well as making plans to set up shop in other locales across the commonwealth. The rivalry, though friendly, was especially fierce at Christmas. Miller & Rhoads' Santa Claus was so popular that shoppers traveled from Virginia's Tidewater and mountain regions, as well as from neighboring states and the District of Columbia, to see the real Santa.

Excited youngsters and their parents waited in long lines outside the store's popular fifth-floor Tea Room for the opportunity to dine with Santa and his beautiful Snow Queen. Celebrated local musician Eddie Weaver filled the air with carols he played simultaneously on the keyboards of a Hammond organ and a spinet piano.

Afterward, making his grand entrance by climbing down a chimney, to the delight of young and old alike, jolly old Saint Nick arrived in the store's seventh-floor Santaland. Once seated in his beautiful antique chair opposite the Snow Queen, Santa miraculously managed to greet each child by name as he or she approached his outstretched arms, climbed into his lap and discussed the specifics of his or her Christmas list. For generations of Virginians, photos of themselves and their children posed with the Miller & Rhoads Santa remain treasured family heirlooms. It made no difference that Thalhimers' Santa made his much-heralded annual arrival into Richmond aboard a gleaming float amid a mile-long procession of high school bands, baton-twirling majorettes and local celebrities in the city's festive illuminated toy parade. Thalhimers executives were the first to admit that nothing they did ever trumped the marketing of the Miller & Rhoads Santa Claus.

Although townsfolk and residents of surrounding Hanover County affectionately referred to "Mr. Cox's store" as the "Miller & Rhoads of Ashland," it had no Santa Claus. "Tiny tots with their eyes all aglow" did not stand in line to reveal their Christmas wish lists to the visitor from the North Pole or have their pictures snapped with him in that store. In 1955, however, someone decided that Santa should make an appearance. Someone also ordained that Santa ought to appropriately make his grand entrance to Ashland on a train. (After all, this was a town where one's ability to keep appointments was largely determined by the passage of lumbering freight trains or gleaming Florida-bound streamliners.) That someone was most certainly Jacqueline Andrews.

The principal organizers, having long since passed on to their glory, are no longer able to testify on their own behalf. Thus, we have been led on a delightful and exciting scavenger hunt for clues surrounding the origins of this central Virginia tradition, whose epicenter appears to be "the center of the universe," as a past mayor of Ashland, the late Richard Gillis, dubbed it. Our journey involved countless hours combing through newspaper microfilm at Randolph-Macon College's McGraw-Page

Library, aided by associate professor Laurie Preston. It also meant knocking on doors to be graciously welcomed into some of Ashland's most beautiful and prestigious homes to examine handcrafted scrapbooks and visit with descendants of the Cox and Andrews families, their friends and neighbors. Additionally, it meant feasting on the culinary wonders of the Iron Horse Restaurant (which incidentally now occupies the one-hundred-year-old, two-story brick building that once was the Cox department store). Indeed, as we turned every corner, our curiosity peaked, especially regarding Mrs. Andrews and the origins of the acclaimed Cox store.

"Jacqueline was a woman ahead of her time, an innovator," according to Ashland resident Sumpter Priddy Jr., himself a legendary Virginian. "I have no doubt whatsoever that the concept of Santa arriving in Ashland by train was hers."[11]

"Oh, I'm sure it was my mother's idea," smiled Cecile Andrews Cox. "And she was a determined woman."[12]

The call from Ashland was made. Most likely, the voice on the other end of the line was Eugene "Gene" Luck, sitting at his desk in the office of the director of passenger service for the Richmond, Fredericksburg & Potomac Railroad at Broad Street Station. The year 1955 was a game-changing one for both of them. Like Mrs. Andrews, Luck was just settling into his responsibilities as the man whose challenge was to reverse the downward trend in passenger ridership that had plagued every U.S. railroad since the end of World War II. But the planets had aligned, as they sometimes do, and something miraculous was about to happen.

Indeed, the RF&P could accommodate the jolly ol' elf. After consulting the railroad's current public timetable, it was agreed that Santa would be taken by automobile to Doswell, about ten miles north of Ashland. There, he would board the RF&P's southbound local passenger train, Number 93. Its schedule would allow him to detrain at Ashland promptly at 11:15 a.m. While railroads in those days were not known to tolerate the slightest of unnecessary delay to their passenger trains, since it was a local—stopping at every pig path and hamlet along the way, as most travelers were convinced—the delay at Ashland could be reasonably justified. After all, like the Cox store, the RF&P was very much a family business.

It was explained that Cox would be taking out ads in the local newspaper, the *Herald-Progress*, so there was likely to be a crowd on hand. How much of a crowd wasn't certain. The 1950 U.S. Census indicated Ashland had a population of 2,106. The store hoped they would all show up on the anticipated Saturday morning. At any rate, the railroad made calls to its operating department to ensure that Number 93's engineer and conductor, as well as the crews of other trains that might be approaching the area, would be alert for persons on or near the tracks at Ashland and act accordingly for safety's sake.

But who would be the Cox Santa?

The renowned Miller & Rhoads Santa Claus was a Hollywood actor. At $1,000 a week in 1942, a national magazine cited him as "the world's highest paid Santa Claus."[13]

Cox obviously didn't have that kind of money to offer. But after planning such a feat of yuletide pageantry, the event couldn't be entrusted to a Santa Claus who'd be nothing more than some farcical high school senior or college freshman, some kid with a beard loosely hanging from his ears to cover a boyish face and a bed pillow wedged into the waistband of his red pajamas, marching around haughtily in a pair of black rubber galoshes, yodeling, "Ho! Ho! Ho!" at the top of a tinny nasal voice that betrayed a recent skirmish with puberty. No, not for Cox Incorporated. No, indeed!

The decision was made to go with a college man, but this college man was no pledge being rushed for a Randolph-Macon fraternity. Baltimore native Robert S. Jeffers was an educator who relocated to Ashland in the early 1950s, serving as the principal of Montpelier High School. He was named president of Smithdeal-Massey Business College in Richmond, where he remained until the proliferation of community colleges forced the small Grace Street institute to shutter its doors in the 1970s. Jeffers, who loved to cook, earned his ultimate claim to fame when he put aside his books and opened the doors of Ashland's "Smokey Pig" barbecue on Washington Highway, where he remained the proprietor until 2004.[14] It was a favorite of *Today Show* host Matt Lauer when the young broadcaster produced local segments of *PM Magazine* in the studios of Richmond ABC-TV affiliate, WXEX, Channel 8.[15]

Bob Jeffers, Ashland's beloved Santa, has also passed away, but the mere mention of his name evokes smiles and pleasant memories from Ashlanders. His daughter, Gwen Jeffers Downey, born after her father's days as Santa Claus for the Cox store, recalled him as "a big man who loved children."

What made him special? "He had an especially nice voice," she smiled. "Not too deep. Playing Santa came very naturally for him, and he greatly enjoyed the role."[16]

Santa Bob anxiously prepared for his debut. In the *Herald-Progress*, the Cox ads proclaimed that Santa would be arriving at the RF&P Station in Ashland on the 11:15 a.m. train on Saturday, November 26. Everyone was invited to meet him at the depot and escort him across the street to the store, where he'd be available to meet with children and pose for pictures every Saturday until Christmas from 10:00 a.m. to 12:00 p.m. and from 1:00 p.m. to 3:00 p.m., as well as every day of Christmas week.[17]

One can only imagine the looks on the passengers' faces aboard RF&P train Number 93 on the morning when Santa Claus climbed aboard for a trip to Richmond. Back then, the arrival of the local passenger train usually created quite a stir anyway. For an hour or so, the sleepy little towns came to life, activity climaxed with the sounding of a distant horn, the sighting of a headlight, the screeching of the steel brake shoes, the thud of the mechanical steps dropping into place and the sound of the conductor's step box hitting the ground. Where an hour before a chorus of crickets would have been deafening, there was suddenly a whirlwind of young children, old folks, station porters and well-wishers, laughing, sobbing, hugging, kissing, shouting and whispering. Mail was put aboard, and boxes containing everything from strawberries to small engine parts were left to the care and handling of the station agent. With a wave between the crew members, the conductor shouted, "All aboard!" stepped up into the vestibule and tugged twice on the cord above his head, signaling the engineer to depart. With two acknowledging, "toots" from the engine horn as its bell clanged, the escaping air from the brakes faded. As they were freed from restraint, the iron wheels gripped the shiny rail and began to rotate. With a slight lurch, the train was

Santa walked from the Ashland train depot (center) to the Cox department store (far left) in 1955 and 1956. Photo circa 1948. *Courtesy Ashland Museum.*

set into motion. The flagman, positioned at the door of the rear car, waved as he watched to ensure no one attempted to board or jump off as the diesel locomotive's engine whined and cast off a bit of exhaust. Seconds later, the two red eyes of the kerosene marker lanterns seemed to wink as the train turned into the sunrise and disappeared from sight. The parking lot cleared, a young father retrieved a flattened penny from the top of the rail, handing it to his young son, and they, too, headed home. Soon, there was nothing moving except a stray dog, sniffing the air for the scent of a morsel of food accidentally dropped on the ground.

Other trains would speed by, destined for stations hundreds of miles away, some laden with freight, others with passengers relaxing in their seats or sipping cups of warm coffee, anticipating their arrivals the next morning in the sunny climes of Georgia, the Carolinas or Florida. The local passenger train would return the next day, though, with the same crew and some of the same passengers.

On November 26, 1955, however, southbound Number 93 was a special train. In the cab of blue, gray and gold RF&P locomotive 1009, the engineer and fireman began scanning the horizon for crowds that were anticipated to be waiting at the Ashland station for a very extraordinary guest—the one who boarded at Doswell—Santa Claus. And they were not disappointed.

According to the following week's *Herald-Progress*, a sea of people, estimated to number into the hundreds, was packed shoulder to shoulder from the crossing at College Avenue, spilling out into the adjacent street that curves around the brick depot.[18] Applying the brakes and easing off the throttle notch-by-notch, the engineer waited for the second of two blasts on the communicating signal from the conductor, telling him when to make a complete stop. No horns were blown in Ashland. Special instructions contained in the employee timetable forbade it. The town and the railroad agreed that except in an emergency, sounding the horn would constitute an unnecessary disturbance.

Opening the locomotive cab door, the fireman joined the engineer, who opened his side window, peering back toward the door that was opened by Number 93's conductor. Before they could even see his fur-trimmed hat and white beard, the gathering of the young and the young at heart let out a cheer that announced to the world that Santa Claus had arrived in Ashland. As he waded into the crowd, the conductor checked to make sure that all other business was accomplished, stepped aboard and again gave the overhead communicating cord two tugs. But this time, he leaned out the top half of coach 522's Dutch door and, with a gentle up and down hand signal,

Santa arrives in Ashland while Gene Luck scans the event from the RF&P Cox Santa Special, November 26, 1955. *Betty Carol Stevenson Private Collection.*

indicated to the engineer to proceed slowly, to make certain that this joyous occasion didn't accidentally turn tragic. Number 93 terminated in Richmond. It was on time, and the engineer knew that with a bit of judicious throttle handling, he could make up the couple of lost minutes resulting from this long Ashland station stop.

As the rear of the train cleared England Street, the conductor again signaled the engineer—this time with a rapid up-and-down hand signal—instructing the engineer to "pick 'em up, and let's get out of here." Their job was done. Ahead lay the end of their run at Broad Street Station. There was also turkey at home to look forward to, left over from Thanksgiving dinner. It would make a nice sandwich.

At the depot, Santa wound his way through the throngs of adoring children and thankful parents. Two sets of eyes watched from a distance. One set, no doubt, watched from the second-floor window of Cox department store. The other peered from the top of an open vestibule door of one of the coaches of train Number 93. Both were calculating, thinking, wondering.

The former set belonged to Jacqueline Andrews. Just as she believed it would, the arrival of jolly ol' Saint Nick flooded the streets of Ashland with potential Cox customers. They came through the front doors, where she hoped they would spy items that they would take home with them or return later to purchase as Christmas gifts. Either way, it was only 11:30 a.m., and it had already been a good day. She must have thought, "He has brought the crowds to Cox. He will bring the entire Ashland community together."

"Santa Claus," she must have thought.

The latter pair of eyes belonged to Gene Luck, who made an attempt to be present for every special move involving an RF&P passenger train. A firm believer in the product he sold, he was satisfied that the Richmond, Fredericksburg & Potomac Railroad performed admirably, even flawlessly. The couple of minutes it perhaps lost at Ashland were of little consequence. Later, in fact, he would write a memo to the head of the operations department (and copy it off to the employee who was responsible for publishing the monthly company newsletter, *Rail-O-Gram*), noting that Number 93's conductor's delay report contained an unusual item—detraining Santa Claus at Ashland. But the little wheels were already turning in Gene Luck's head as he watched those hundreds of people greet Santa before the train swept past them leaving Ashland. How could he make those hundreds of people RF&P passenger train patrons?

"Santa Claus," he must have thought.

CHAPTER 3

HOP ABOARD

Gene Luck had apparently passed the test. He'd promised to resign after a period of six months if he did not satisfactorily fulfill his new role of marketing the Richmond, Fredericksburg & Potomac Railroad's passenger service. It was now 1957, two years later, and no one had shown up to take his name off the office door or escort him out of Broad Street Station.

To the contrary, Luck had endeared himself to the RF&P's management and operating personnel. They saw him as an energetic cheerleader, someone rooting for the home team, a man actively soliciting passenger business at a time when other railroads had thrown in the towel. Luck's philosophy was that one person's failure was simply an opportunity for another to succeed—especially one with ideas, and he had lots of those.

Nationwide, railroad passenger traffic continued to decline, due in large part to the ability of returning wartime servicemen to purchase automobiles for use on the country's rapidly improving array of streets and highways. Adding insult to injury, it didn't help that income from first-class and Pullman Company corporate travel was eroding, as businessmen began purchasing plane tickets in preference to sleeping-car space. Understandably, most railroad companies were seeking ways to rid themselves of the costly burden of providing the public with passenger trains, if not actively seeking ways to discourage people from riding.

Not even Gene Luck saw much of a future for the local passenger train. While Luck explored new ways to increase patronage on the railroad's crack limiteds and special trains, the RF&P was applying to the Virginia and

Interstate Commerce Commissions to relieve it from operating "milk runs," as they were jokingly dubbed. They earned that name because at one time, these trains stopped to pick up dairy products from the hinterlands and convey them into the city. Local passenger trains trundled up and down the main line from one obscure village to the next, sometimes hauling fewer passengers than crew—and seldom, if ever, did they actually carry milk anymore. Their slow, plodding pace and decreasing frequencies made them low-hanging fruit for motor coach operators. The family auto made a much more attractive alternative. The RF&P had, in fact, successfully just been granted authority to discontinue north- and southbound locals, Numbers 10 and 29, respectively, as of January 12, 1957.

Luck had high hopes for the highly touted Blue & Gray Clipper trains, which promised to speed patrons between Richmond and Washington "in under two hours for under five bucks," when they premiered in 1955. To that end, the RF&P's newest and best equipment was utilized; its diner was ready to serve prior to its morning departure from Broad Street Station and its evening return from Washington Union Station. Passengers found mints, magazines and the latest newspapers at their seats. To ensure on-time performance, the railroad had increased the Clipper train's speed to eighty miles per hour for a running time of one hour and fifty-nine minutes, or less (and that included intermediate stops at Ashland, Fredericksburg, Quantico and Alexandria).

But as William E. Griffin noted in his excellent comprehensive history of RF&P passenger service between 1935 and 1975, Luck's chief belief was that people would flock to buy train tickets when they were purchased in conjunction with a planned event or as part of a group—or both.[19] To that end, he began planning evening excursions to Washington for theatrical performances, with dinner served en route, capped by a quick return trip to Richmond. Show tickets were included. By partnering with the Pennsylvania Railroad, patrons could arrange for a five-night Broadway package, complete with convenient Manhattan hotel rooms. The lowly Washington Redskins were happy to provide Luck with as many tickets as he wished in order to lure NFL fans aboard the trains for the price of a round-trip ticket to Union Station, allowing him to return those that went unsold. Bus transportation between Union Station and Griffith Stadium was also included in the package price. (The RF&P eventually ended up with a block of six hundred Redskins season tickets, worth their weight in gold after Coach George Allen some years later made contenders out of what had been the worst team in the league.)

Everyone, it seemed, wanted to ride Gene Luck's RF&P special trains, even the Cox Incorporated Santa Claus. The image of those hundreds of people waiting to greet Santa as he alighted from Number 93 at Ashland for the past two Christmas seasons still lingered fresh in his mind.

"Why not let the kids (and their parents, of course) join him?" he surely thought.

Young children had a fascination with trains—as did an awful lot of grownups. Luck had proved it in 1956, when he put together a diesel-powered special consisting of fifteen RF&P caboose cars and a couple of passenger coaches. The first father-and-son "Caboose Train" left Richmond's Acca Yard and traveled north to the home of the U.S. Marines, Quantico, Virginia, through which the RF&P's tracks conveniently ran. Everyone took turns, riding one way in a storied "little red caboose," while on the return trip, in the opposite direction, they were seated in a comfortable air-conditioned coach car. Once on the base, the young boys and their dads were feted to a thrilling demonstration of the leathernecks' military skills, as well as a parade featuring the Marine Corps Marching Band. The visitors' activities culminated in sharing chow right there in the base mess hall before boarding their homebound train. To top it all, each bright-eyed youngster was given a genuine, pinstriped railroad cap on which was affixed a patch sporting the official RF&P logo—just like real railroaders wore. What a treat!

The railroad's collaboration with Cox's department store had been a rousing success for two years now—at least for the merchant. True, Cox had gone to the expense of advertising the event. The second year, according to the *Herald-Progress*, the awaiting crowd at Ashland had grown to an estimated one thousand people—mathematically, nearly half the town's entire population. But for the RF&P, it really wasn't a revenue producer. It's uncertain whether Santa even paid for his own ticket.

Supposing there were a special train large enough to accommodate crowds of that size, just arranging for the equipment would be a bit more daunting than finding a few idle wooden caboose cars and a spare freight locomotive or two, as was the case with the father-son caboose train outing on a leisurely Saturday morning. No, this would be a far more intricate operation. Not only would it include a great deal of planning, but it also would involve ticket sales, manpower, coordination and a vivid imagination.

Also, it would mean partnering with the small Ashland retailer, convincing it that it could afford to charter an entire train, not just springing for a single ticket from Doswell to Ashland for jolly old Saint Nick. There would need to be something to occupy the children while Santa walked through the train to greet the excited young believers. It would be quite a challenge. It would take someone else with determination and the ability to successfully plan, organize and pull off such an undertaking, but Gene Luck felt that he'd already met her. It's not hard to imagine him picking up his office phone and placing a call to Jacqueline Andrews at Cox Incorporated in Ashland.

For a man who could sell the merits of enhanced passenger train service to RF&P Railroad president W. Thomas Rice Jr., however, nothing was impossible.

CHAPTER 4

WON'T YOU RIDE MY SLEIGH TONIGHT?

Where and when the meeting took place is unknown. Clearly, however, a conversation did ensue between Fairfax Davis and the Andrewses, his two partners at Cox Incorporated. The agenda: how should they proceed with regard to sponsoring a special Santa Claus train for the 1957 holiday season with the Richmond, Fredericksburg & Potomac Railroad, or was it even feasible? After all, they weren't Macy's. (There might indeed have been 8 million stories in *The Naked City*, but at last count, there were just 2,106 souls residing within the corporate limits of Ashland.)[20]

The only Santa-related promotional expense they had incurred in the past two years was to purchase ads in the *Herald-Progress*. Also, they needed to compensate Bob Jeffers, the gentleman who had portrayed Santa as he arrived in Ashland aboard the 11:15 a.m. train and was present in the store to meet with the army of excited children on Saturdays prior to Christmas. Their investment, while minimal, had been prudent—an excellent one, in fact. On those two November days, large crowds flooded the adjacent streets. From all indications, the innovative Cox Santa tradition had been heartily embraced by the citizens of the small college town and surrounding Hanover County. It bolstered a sense of community pride that was ever present there and reflected well on the small Ashland retailer.

Before taking their promotion to the next level, more than doubling down on their wager, they would have to know what was at stake and what would be involved.

Cox Incorporated, the "Miller & Rhoads of Ashland," as it appeared in 1955. *Betty Carol Stevenson Private Collection.*

While they were sure that Miller & Rhoads and Thalhimers had taken note of their holiday marketing coup, it was quite possible the big boys downtown could simply have been distracted by their expansion plans. Commercials already filled the air on radio and television reminding Richmonders that it was only one stop to park and shop at Wonderful Willow Lawn in Henrico County. At the same time, on the south side of the James River, the finishing touches were already being added to another shopping center, Southside Plaza, in Chesterfield County.

The move was a matter of concern for Cox, as well as the smaller merchants in Richmond's Broad and Grace Streets shopping district who benefited from the foot traffic generated by the large retailers, whose seven-floor stores occupied almost two square city blocks. If shoppers abandoned the downtown anchor stores to park free and spend their money in proximity to their new brick ranch-style suburban homes, the small merchants were unsure what would happen to their stores.

Those who could afford to do so hedged their bets by signing leases for space in one or both of the new shopping centers, while keeping one foot inside the downtown retail core. On paper, it looked good. Like the major retailers, they too were "expanding to meet their customers' needs." The cautionary word among shopkeepers was "Don't panic." Once a breakout into the suburbs had been made, however, it was as if permission had been granted for an early dismissal from school. Car dealerships, service stations and restaurants would follow. And as conveniences became more available farther outside of town, new home and apartment construction would follow until it became a leapfrogging contest of which came first, the chicken or the egg.

Of equal concern to Cox were plans to extend the recently opened Richmond–Petersburg Toll Road northward, on a route parallel to U.S. 1. Unlike the four-lane divided highway to the south, it was toll-free. The Interstate Highway System was not some vague pipe dream, no pie in the sky. It was here and now. Plans were already on the drawing boards. Land was being acquired. Surely, an interchange allowing motorists to exit what was announced to be Interstate 95 at State Route 54 was a given—or at least, one would hope so. After all, five miles to the east was Hanover Court House, the seat of government. Just a few blocks away were the businesses that lined U.S. 1 and, beyond them, Ashland's commercial district, as well as the campus of Randolph-Macon College. Ashland wouldn't be bypassed, but that didn't necessarily mean its economy would be spared.

Highway builders were not the only people scooping up parcels of land. Where cloverleaves sprouted like crabgrass, so would modern travel facilities bearing names like Howard Johnson's, Holiday Inn, Esso and Sunoco. Local businesses, close to the big junction, might benefit from the dollars sure to be spent by weary travelers seeking clean rooms, hot meals and tanks of gas. Their competition would be an increasing number of national chains with a voracious appetite to swallow up small-town businesses. The small motor courts, diners and road houses occupying the long stretches of U.S. 1 between interchanges would come to resemble deserted Hollywood back lots. All that would be lacking were tumbleweeds, most of their owners were convinced. And there were no tumbleweeds in Central Virginia.

A lot was on the minds of the Cox Incorporated owners as the pages of the 1957 calendar were ripped away, revealing the following months. At this juncture, though, anything they did had to be carefully calculated and implemented. Otherwise, like the calendar, their days, too, would be numbered.

Rather than using his normal parking spot beside the terminal building at Broad Street Station, this particular morning, Gene Luck drove a block farther east and then turned left, taking the driveway that rose and vaulted above the curving tracks next to the Hot Shoppes restaurant and coming to rest on the opposite side of the boarding platforms and tracks. He didn't stop at the brick building where Railway Express filled and emptied cars loaded with packages and crates that, until the days of UPS and FedEx, moved by scheduled passenger trains. He kept right on past the coal-burning steam heat plant that provided winter warmth for the huge station, past the commissary where supplies were kept for food service cars and even past the very busy two-story tower, where an operator flipped switches and mashed buttons on a huge blinking, lighted display board, directing trains from one track to the other. These were buildings that most travelers never saw or even knew existed.

Luck's destination was a small railroad yard, where idle passenger cars were stored and where others were cleaned and serviced. It was where he intended to examine surplus equipment to see if it would indeed be suitable for use to transport Santa Claus and hundreds of laughing children and their parents for Ashland's Cox department store.

The RF&P primarily forwarded the New York–Florida streamliners of the Atlantic Coast Line and Seaboard Air Line Railroads, as well as trains bound to and from Petersburg and Norfolk, Virginia, operated by the Norfolk & Western Railway. It jointly purchased cars with those railroads to equip them. Still, the RF&P operated a dwindling number of its own trains, locals serving communities between Richmond and Washington—"The Capital Cities Route, Linking North and South"—as its slogan read. As such, it retained a relatively small fleet of older passenger equipment for standby use. The railroad's economy-minded management was already selling off some of it to the railroads of Mexico and South America, which regarded even antiquated American passenger equipment built of steel as though it were another, more precious metal.

Although the RF&P still carried over 1 million passengers annually, those numbers paled in comparison to the traffic the 110-mile railroad had seen during World War II. It recorded 8.5 million passengers in 1943 with 103 scheduled freight and passenger trains—1 every fourteen minutes. One day alone, April 21 of that same year, 131 trains moved between Richmond and Washington. Two days later, a record was set when 33,324 people boarded the line's passenger trains.[21]

Luck felt the presence of the ghost of railroading past as he closed the door of his automobile, walked through the weeds and scanned the long lines of the RF&P's 500-series coach cars. Heavy, by modern standards, constructed of steel in the 1930s, they required six axles to support the eighty-six coach seats that edged their worn linoleum aisles, two by two. They rode like Cadillacs, however. The bulk remained painted in their original dark Pullman green, as they had been when the faces of GIs filled their raised wooden window sashes. Sailors and marines also had boarded them, gladly closing their eyes in the 500s' stiff-backed seats. Some preferred to climb into the overhead baggage racks for some shut-eye during a journey that would end on some battlefield in Europe or Asia. Maybe they'd be headed home, this time battling smoke and cinders as their train marched on to the cadence of a coal-burning steam locomotive.

Twenty of these old coach cars had been air-conditioned and modernized—by 1941 standards, that is. With the delivery of the railroad's first new diesel-electric passenger locomotives in December 1949, they began being painted an attractive matching blue and gray with gold accent stripes. By 1952, the RF&P no longer used steam locomotives, and with its slumping passenger ridership, its recently purchased lightweight passenger equipment amply sufficed to handle regularly scheduled trains. Thus, even the "modernized" 500-series cars were put out to pasture, grazing in the weeds of the Broad Street Station coach yard, their future uncertain.

These would do, though. They'd be run through an inspection to make sure that their steam heat worked, that their toilets flushed and that they were mechanically sound. Like a man who'd just kicked the tires of a used car he'd decided to buy, Gene Luck now jumped back into his car and headed to the offices of the RF&P's chief mechanical officer and operating managers. There he would inquire exactly what would be involved in setting up a train that would make a trip that was short enough to not strain the attention span of preschoolers and first graders yet give Santa an opportunity to walk through the train and visit with each one of them.

"It'll take two E8s, that's for sure," responded the RF&P road foreman of engines—the gentleman who supervised the railroad's roster of locomotive engineers and who knew every foot of track from Richmond to Potomac Yard in Alexandria. "And since there's no place to turn them around, you'll have to run two of them, back to back."

An E8 was a 2,250-horsepower diesel-electric locomotive, designed specially to power passenger trains. They were manufactured just outside Chicago, at the LaGrange, Illinois plant of the Electro Motive Division of General Motors. The front end of an E8 was equipped with a headlight, a horn and a bell, and it was the location where the engineer peered through the windshield and controlled the movement of the train. If two E8 passenger locomotives were operated back to back, it was only necessary for the engineer to move from the controls of one to the controls of the other to change the direction of travel.

What made a passenger locomotive different from its freight counterpart was the presence of a steam generator, located at the opposite end of the E8. It turned water into pressurized steam that was passed back through the train to provide warmth in the winter as well as hot water. (Lights and air conditioning were battery powered.)

The RF&P had only fifteen E8 passenger locomotives with which to operate all of its trains, so it would require a bit of creative scheduling to ensure that there would be two available for the Cox Santa Special.

The suggestion was made that the proposed Santa Train should stop at Ashland, southbound, where it would pick up its youthful passengers. After boarding everyone, it would then come to Richmond, but instead of stopping, it would merely continue through Broad Street Station, past the boarding platforms, around the semicircular loops of track, and thus be headed in the right direction to return to Ashland. Being about a twenty-minute trip in both directions, Santa would have almost an hour to greet and speak with all the boys and girls from Hanover who would climb aboard at Ashland.

The logistics of having the train in position for the special move was a bit more complicated, though. To uncouple the two locomotives from the north end of the train and move them to the south end at Doswell so that the train's direction could be changed to make its grand entrance into Ashland, there would need to be mechanical personnel on hand. The operating crew would consist of an engineer, a fireman, a conductor and at least one other assistant conductor to make all the moves. Since there would be a great number of small children, for safety's sake, there would need to be additional supervisory personnel aboard.

The scope of this small train was beginning to widen. It now included more people and more equipment. All of this meant more money. Just like the folks at Cox Incorporated, some people at the RF&P were beginning to wonder if this train was truly going to leave the station. Gene Luck and Jacqueline Andrews were not among them, however. Both were already on board.

CHAPTER 5

GIRLS' NIGHT OUT

In the weeks and days leading up to the launch of the Cox Incorporated–RF&P Santa Claus Special, a great many details had to be ironed out.

For the railroad's part, it was more a matter of determining how to get crews and equipment in place. After all, this was one of America's oldest railroads, whose origins can be traced back to 1834, when it was granted a charter by the Commonwealth of Virginia to build a line north to the Potomac. The railroad was 110 miles long, but if you included the track and structures that had been rebuilt time and again during the American Civil War as part of the tally, it surely seemed twice that length. The fact that it continued to operate continuously throughout the conflict and was able to resume service to help rebuild the Old Dominion shortly after the last shots were fired is a testament to those who managed and ran it.

Though truncated and dismembered, torn and tattered, burned and rebuilt to be used by armies whose soldiers wore both Union blue and Confederate gray, depending on who controlled the same segment of rail on any given day, it was able to keep on chugging.

Military conflict was not the only battle fought for the RF&P. Initially granted a monopoly to serve that route exclusively, it had to fend off attempts by resourceful financiers, scheming scoundrels and empire builders who combined in attempts to outflank it. One such attempt resulted in a parallel rail line that extended from Richmond to Ashland, before the ploy was stopped dead in its tracks. It later served as an interurban railway and, finally, a trolley line before its owners abandoned the rails and used the right of way for electrical transmission. With such a rich history behind it, operating a special train to serve as Santa's sleigh for a single day was hardly an insurmountable obstacle.

While having seen to the needs of the population of Ashland for nearly one hundred years, the new owners of Cox's were not adept at staging such large-scale promotions. To be sure, it wasn't as simple as merely taking out a few ads in the *Herald-Progress* and persuading Bob Jeffers to dress in his Santa costume to ride the train a bit farther this year. Whereas Saint Nick had been dropped off the train to start a party at the front door of Cox Incorporated for the past two years, this year—Friday night, December 6, it had been decided—the party would not only begin and end in Ashland but would also continue on board a moving train with Santa for almost an hour in between. Anyone who has ever served as host for a child's birthday party knows that no matter how many games and activities you plan or how much cake and ice cream you serve, there is never enough. Because of children's short attention spans, there has to be something exciting going on every minute.

There would be clowns and Christmas songs to keep each child entertained until Santa arrived in his or her car. There would be candy and presents to be distributed. Simple. But where would the clowns come from? Who would play the music? How would the candy and trinkets be distributed?

Joe Andrews had just heard back from Gene Luck. Based on the estimated one thousand people who showed up to greet Santa the previous year, the RF&P was suggesting that it operate an eleven-car train, using some of its best 500-series coaches. Because it was a Friday, when children would have been in school all day, the plan was to have the Cox Santa Special arrive in Ashland in time enough to depart for Richmond at 7:30 p.m. It would be a nonstop round trip that would deliver Santa and his young charges back to the Ashland depot at about 8:30 p.m., just in time for the youngsters to be taken home to say their prayers and be tucked into bed. The railroad would have to position the train north of town, at Doswell, for the trip into Richmond and back, and it would have to return the engines and cars to Broad Street Station. The mechanics of the train operation seemed to be worked out accordingly. Although it isn't known how much Cox Incorporated agreed to pay the RF&P to operate the train, the fare was to be twenty-five cents for each adult and child.

From Gene Luck's standpoint, this was going to be an opportunity to introduce future RF&P patrons and their parents to the excitement of train travel in the hope that it would become habit forming. It was like the practice of a local Richmond barbecue establishment, catering to teens and young adults with an affinity for cruising the restaurant's locations on weekend and summer nights in their cars, with the tops down, playing music and having fun. The owner provided each high school class president and service organization in town with special identification cards, entitling them to a free sandwich and limeade each week. Knowing that impressionable youths were constantly involved in a real life game of follow the leader, he'd make his money back hundreds of times over when the top students' friends came along for the ride and ended up paying for their barbecues and sodas.

Luck believed in his product. Train travel excited him, and he loved sharing the experience, even if it was his job to sell tickets, although, in this instance, the RF&P would not be selling any. It only made sense that the sole location to obtain tickets for the Cox Incorporated Santa Special be a special ticket booth on the first floor at Cox's department store. Joe Andrews himself got into the spirit of the event by donning a conductor's hat and coat just to be photographed for an ad that appeared in the *Herald-Progress* promoting the train. Red ribbons that read, "December 6th is the day," were handed out and worn by everyone in town.

In the short two years that Santa had begun arriving in Ashland and walking across the street to Cox's, a tradition had been born. When word spread that this year, Santa was inviting all of his young friends to come join him riding the train, it became the talk of the town.

"Everyone was talking about it," recalled Sarah Wright. "All my friends were planning on going with their children. Everybody wanted to be a part of it. It was Christmas, and you wanted to ride the Santa Train."[22]

As for manning the cars on the train for the Santa Special, Miller & Rhoads had more supervisors in a single department than Cox had employees on its payroll. It was a small store taking on a huge endeavor; but the town had come to expect it, and the folks at Cox's weren't going to disappoint them.

Whereas a large business could simply direct some of its workers to do the company's bidding, Cox Incorporated would have to call out volunteers. That didn't bother Jacqueline Andrews, though. She had a network of friends in Ashland with high school–aged daughters. Miller & Rhoads' Santa might have had a Snow Queen to aid Santa at its Tea Room and Santaland, but the Cox Santa Special would have a Fairy Princess reigning over each car in the train. With a bevy of beauties who attended the prom at Henry Clay High School, she'd see to it. Once again, she picked up the phone.

CHAPTER 6

IT'S SHOWTIME!

If anyone had any doubts about the success of the Cox Santa Special, their hang-ups immediately dissipated soon after the first ads appeared in the November 1957 editions of the *Herald-Progress*. Hazel Moore, an Ashland resident, once worked at the Cox store. She recalled the crowds awaiting the first demonstration of the modern marvel of television there in 1948, when WTVR began transmitting on Channel 6 from Richmond. Nine years later, while Santa Special customers were not jamming the sales floor as customers had that first night of broadcast history, there was a steady stream of moms and pops shelling out twenty-five cents for each ticket they purchased to ride the December 6 much-talked-about "Santa Train."[23]

The ads stated that there would be a limit of one thousand tickets available, requiring an eleven-car train. Quickly, however, it was apparent that the limit would be reached in a matter of days.[24]

Joe Andrews had envisioned purchases of two, three or four tickets for families who wished to spend the evening together aboard the train with Old Saint Nick. You can imagine his surprise when one of the ladies in town anxiously showed up when the store opened the next day, opening her purse to hand over several crisp dollar bills, asking for enough Santa tickets to accommodate the members of her bridge club and their children. The first Saturday night after the promotion was announced in the Thursday *Herald-Progress*, a weather-worn old farmer appeared, reached into his bib overalls, pulled out a wad of green, licked his thumb and peeled off three equally well-worn dollar bills, asking for a dozen tickets.

A rare promotional ribbon for the first Cox Santa Special, 1957. *Cecile Andrews Cox Private Collection.*

It was no longer just a family affair. This was going to be an event. People were buying tickets for themselves, their neighbors, Sunday school classes and fraternal groups. In some cases, they had invited friends and family from out of town to pack up the kids and head for Ashland to jump-start their enjoyment of the holiday season. Others were driving down from Ruther Glen, Beaverdam and Ladysmith. Andrews had to be wondering if he was running a department store or a travel agency.

With the first one thousand tickets having vanished almost overnight, another call was made to Gene Luck. Could the RF&P accommodate more than the projected one thousand riders? He responded that he'd consult the railroad's mechanical department and get back with an answer as soon as possible.

Luck had pitched the idea of the Santa Train after seeing the thousand or so greeters who had met Number 93 for the past two years when Santa rode it into town. But even he was surprised at how quickly the available seats for this special train were selling out. The last thing he wanted to do was create a scenario that turned a goodwill gesture into a bitter disappointment for lots of young boys and girls. Such an undesirable result, with no stretch of the imagination, would anger parents, who would have to explain to their sons or daughters why Santa couldn't see them.

He picked up his office phone and began making inquiries. Of the twenty 500-series coaches, how many would be travel worthy and thus available for use on the sixth? If so, would there be enough locomotives available to power a longer, heavier train? After all, these were "heavy weight" cars, made of steel, not the newer, lighter streamlined coaches that equipped most of the speedy limiteds and through trains the RF&P handled in 1957.

It should have been no surprise to Luck when he was told that all twenty coach cars could be available for the excursion and that if there were to be a shortage, one or two of the more streamlined 700-series coaches would possibly be idle and thus available to be pressed into service. Additional motive power, if needed, would pose no problem.

Luck smiled as he hung up the phone and then dialed what was becoming a very familiar number in Ashland. If necessary, he explained to owners Andrews and Davis, there could be as many as twenty-two coaches, seating roughly 2,300 people. That number, however, he warned, could not be surpassed.

After putting the receiver back in its cradle, for a brief moment, Joe Andrews seemed relieved as yet another customer approached him asking for a half dozen tickets. Happily, now he was able to grant her request without the least hesitation.

Suddenly, there was an empty feeling in the pit of his stomach. Twenty-two passenger cars filled with children and adults—2,300 people? That was more than Ashland's entire population. He wasn't about to complain. After all, this was Cox Incorporated's goal. But who was going to help manage the crowd, direct traffic and board everyone on the train? Had he bitten off more than he, his wife and his business partner could chew?

Suddenly, a promotion by this small-town merchant had snowballed into a likely scenario for a Frank Capra film—one that the fabled director would have dearly loved to have scripted and directed—a phenomenon that could happen only in a small American town.

At that moment, the Cox Incorporated Santa Special had become Ashland's Santa Train. Somehow it seemed the right time for Mickey Rooney and Judy Garland to come charging into the store and, recognizing the existence of a dilemma, shout out, "We know the answer; let's put on a show!" There was, in fact, already going to be a show, but at this point, the challenge was going to be finding a cast and crew to present it—one large enough to pull it off. Joseph and Jacqueline Andrews and Fairfax Davis would obviously have to look beyond the doors of their store for help. In a town as close knit as Ashland, they felt sure some people would step forward, but whether there would be enough was another matter. They'd ask their friends and neighbors.

Jacqueline Andrews alternated between thoughts of delight and anxiety. She'd initially promised the railroad that there would be a sufficient number of young ladies to fulfill the roles of hostess, or Fairy Princess, in each car, eleven total. Now, there would need to be as many as twenty-two. She stopped for a moment, however, and allowed herself the luxury of closing her eyes to imagine the splendor of seeing her beautiful daughter, Cecile, in her prom gown, a scepter in her hand and a tiara atop her head, gracing the aisle of the train as if she were striding the runway of a fashion show.

Cecile Andrews Cox (she later married Jim Cox, grandson of the store's founder) was kind enough to invite Doug Riddell into her beautiful Ashland home recently to pore through the pages of her scrapbook. Contained between its pages were souvenirs from her reign as a Fairy Princess aboard the Santa Special. The tiaras worn by her and her friends were lovingly

Fairy Princess Lanie Covington Turnage, Cox Train in 1957. *Middle row, from left to right*: Suzanne Huff, Stephanie Huff, Jerre Huff, Nelson Taylor Jr. and Mae Taylor. *Suzanne Huff Private Collection. Nelson Taylor Sr., photographer.*

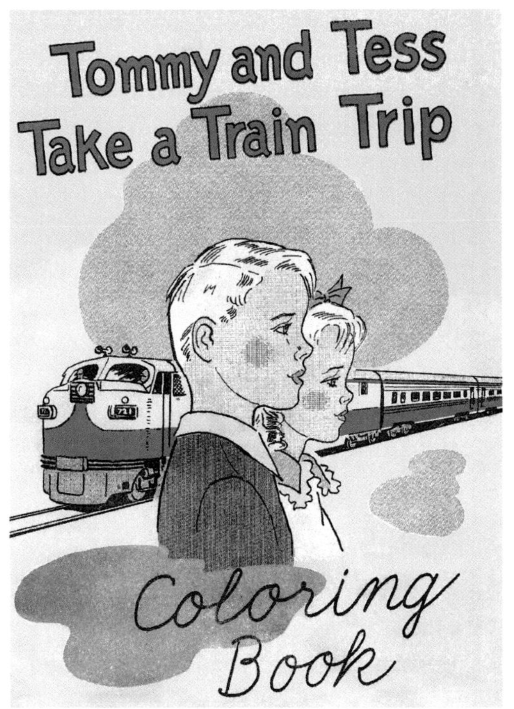

Tommy and Tess Take a Train Trip coloring book was distributed by the Fairy Princesses aboard the Cox Santa Special, 1957 and 1958. *Cecile Andrews Cox Private Collection.*

handcrafted from cardboard and aluminum foil, sprinkled with red and blue glitter to give them a regal glow. The scepters they carried were wooden dowels, to which cardboard stars, immersed in silver glitter, were affixed. They would also wear wings, which gave them an apparent ability to flitter from one end of their coach car to the other but in reality prevented them from being able to sit down.[25] The glow on the young ladies' faces, the sparkle in their eyes and the smiles that stretched from cheek to cheek, were theirs and theirs alone—a priceless treasure in any realm.

"I wish I had a better copy of this picture of my father," Mrs. Cox said, looking at the faded newspaper ad showing Joe Andrews in his railroad hat, clipped from the pages of the *Herald-Progress*. It was torn across the bottom portion and, as such, unusable as an illustration for the book you're holding. "I tried to keep everything, including one of the lollypops we were handing out. Unfortunately, over the years in the attic, it melted, and everything got all sticky."[26]

Another item from her Santa Claus Special collection was a thin coloring book, *Tommy and Tess Take a Train Trip*. Produced by the Association of American Railroads (AAR), it was distributed through its members as a means of introducing youngsters to the world of trains. Gene Luck made them available to be given away along with candy on the Santa Trains. Mrs. Cox's copy had fallen victim to the same melted lollypop but was salvageable through the marvel of modern digital technology.

Another 1957 Fairy Princess was Betty Carol Stevenson, who remembered, "We were all attending Henry Clay High School when Mrs. Andrews asked us to participate in the first Santa Train to host children and their parents. We felt so honored to be chosen." Mrs. Stevenson noted that Jacqueline Andrews herself made the accessories. Over the years, the Fairy Princesses have remained friends—most still living in the Ashland area; some in or near the same homes in which they lived at the time of that first train ride.

"There was Mary Anna Tignor Sylvia, Cecile Andrews Cox and Lanie Covington Turnage. And there are others; I can't remember how many or all of their names, but there was one for each car," Mrs. Stevenson remembered.[27]

Joe Andrews's worries were short lived. By the night of December 6, even with a twenty-two car train, he had a full complement of friends, associates and neighbors who simply were caught up in the excitement of what most local folks nostalgically regard as the most major event of any holiday season in Ashland.

In its Thursday, December 5 edition, the *Herald-Progress* boasted that fully twenty-six Henry Clay High School students would be participating in the festivities. Five men from Ashland would be decked out as clowns. Of course, Bob Jeffers would be reprising his role as Ashland's beloved Santa.[28]

Long before the sun set that Friday night, the engineers and conductors who would operate the Santa Special were called by the RF&P crew dispatcher and informed when to sign up for duty. The long train had been assembled at Broad Street Station. The two diesel-electric locomotives that would power it were attached.

Betty Carol Stevenson recalls that the Fairy Princesses were driven to Richmond to board the train along with Santa. Departing Broad Street Station, a straight run would be made to Doswell. To the crowd of hundreds already gathering at the Ashland depot, the idea was for the train slipping through town to appear no different than any of the other scores of RF&P passenger trains that roared down the middle of Railroad Avenue every day of the year. Santa, the clowns and the Fairy Princesses were careful not to be near a window where they would be noticed. Santa was supposed to be coming from "the North Pole—not Richmond."[29]

Once at Doswell, the locomotives were detached from the north end of the train, operated to the opposite end and recoupled, so as to be properly headed south. Along with the engineer and fireman, Santa Bob Jeffers climbed into the locomotive cab. When they arrived in Ashland, he'd open the door to wave at the crowd, which now was lining the tracks on the west side of the entire length of Railroad Avenue, from Patrick to Thompson Streets—two long blocks.

With all of the air and steam connections made and inspected by the small army of mechanics and pipe fitters, the train's conductor was given charge of the Santa Special. Noting a green light to proceed south, he signaled the engineer to begin the ten-minute journey to Ashland, reminding him beforehand to approach the town very slowly because of the expected crowds waiting to catch a glimpse of the jolly ol' elf as they arrived.

While operating department supervisors saw to the details, Gene Luck was in charge of the move, and a bit like an expectant father, he was to oversee the birth of a tradition. He wanted everything to go smoothly, and it did.

Hanover and Ashland law enforcement officers were in place, keeping traffic moving and preventing the curious from getting too close to the tracks. While the main event of the night was the Santa Special, there were other trains—both freight and passenger—that would need to use the other track. Undoubtedly, Joe and Jacqueline Andrews were on the platform, as was Fairfax Davis, when someone, noting a brightening of the northern sky, shouted out, "Here comes Santa Claus!"

According to the *Herald-Progress* account carried in the following week's edition, Hunter McAlister, of the Ashland Rescue Squad, took to the public address system to announce the train's arrival and to urge caution as it approached the depot. The Henry Clay High School band struck up a stirring rendition of "Santa Claus Is Coming to Town," the crowd began to shout and sing and, as if by magic, the chimes atop the First National Bank began to peal.[30] As the big blue and gray RF&P locomotive halted just short of the crossing in front of the station, Santa opened the door and waved. "Merry Christmas, and all aboard!" was the greeting some claimed he shouted.

The streets were festooned with strings of Christmas lights, hanging from side to side, as was the annual custom in Ashland. Norman Rockwell was surely present somewhere nearby. If he wasn't, it was his misfortune, because this indeed was how he intended to portray Christmas in Middle America on the holiday covers of the *Saturday Evening Post.*

With such a large number of people attempting to board the train, the two engines and twenty-two cars stood idling for over an hour, despite the efforts of Cox employees, railroad officials and anyone who could be enlisted to lift the small children up the steps and down the aisles. Finally, at just before 9:00 p.m., the bell on the lead locomotive began to sound, the headlight again shone bright and, with a smoothness that eluded detection, the train began moving south toward Richmond.

On board, a clown, Bill Ayres, and a Fairy Princess, Linda Moore, began singing Christmas songs as they moved through the first of many cars, handing out lollypops to children, many of whom were making their very first train trip. According to future Ashland mayor Dick Gillis, another Fairy Princess, sixteen-year-old Henry Clay junior Jerriane Redford, began visiting with each youngster in her car.[31]

Suddenly, the door to the car opened, and a small brass combo from the Henry Clay High School band broke out in "Jingle Bells," followed by "Santa Claus Is Coming to Town." Of course, upon hearing his theme song, Santa burst through the door with a jolly "Ho, Ho, Ho" to the delight of everyone within earshot.

"We weren't paid anything," laughed Betty Carol Stevenson, "but we would have paid them for the privilege of serving as Fairy Princesses."[32]

The trip was billed as a nonstop round-trip journey from Ashland to Richmond and back. After only about ten minutes, the train began to slow down, passing the multicolored signals, and the white lanterns waved at the Santa Special as it navigated its way through busy Acca Yard. It then began to curve through a loop of track that led it into, through and out of Broad Street Station, headed back for Ashland.

Imagine, if you will, being quietly seated in a coach on the Miami-bound East Coast Champion, preparing for departure and peering outside your window to see a train gliding by. Through those windows you catch a glimpse of frolicking children, dancing clowns, musicians and Santa Claus. An odd sight, one might conclude, but it's the Christmas season. Before you can take it all in, the last car disappears into the curtain of darkness that is nighttime in December in the Old Dominion, and you're thinking, "These Virginians, they certainly do enjoy the holidays."

Instructions had been given to the train crew to attempt to allow Santa to make an appearance throughout the entire train, so the engineer and his fireman in the cab of their locomotive relaxed a bit, not compelled this night to press hard to keep a schedule that meant pushing their engines to the max to maintain passenger train speeds. With twenty-two cars in tow, that was probably a blessing, because even with two fairly new and powerful locomotives, the weight of the train made any attempt at high-speed travel almost impossible.

Trains entering and departing Broad Street Station in Richmond used the loop of track shown in this aerial view, circa 1960. *Courtesy RF&P Railroad Historical Society.*

What was important was that each child would get to see Santa, as Gene Luck had impressed on the RF&P employees working the train.

"Bob Jeffers had big rosy cheeks and a kind eye. He did such a good job," recalled Sumpter Priddy Jr. of that night in 1957. "The children were so excited. You could see their little eyes dance!"[33]

For Fairy Princess Mary Anna Tignor Sylvia, it was a wondrous night—magical, you might say. "She gently touched the top of a little girl's head with her magic wand," remembered Betty Carol Stevenson, "telling her indeed, that it was magic. It seemed that every child in her car saw this, so she had to go up and down the aisle, touching each child on the head with her wand."[34]

Reporter (and later mayor of Ashland) Dick Gillis quoted the summation of his own five-year-old daughter, Kim, in the *Herald-Progress*: "It was wonderful, and Santa is so nice."[35]

On the porches of the homes facing the RF&P tracks at Ashland, as well as on the sidewalks of Railroad Avenue, the people of this very special little town shouted and waved as the long train slowed down and eased its way to a stop at the station platform, less than an hour after this mystical journey to the North Pole had begun. It was nearly 10:00 p.m. Tiny tots, even some of

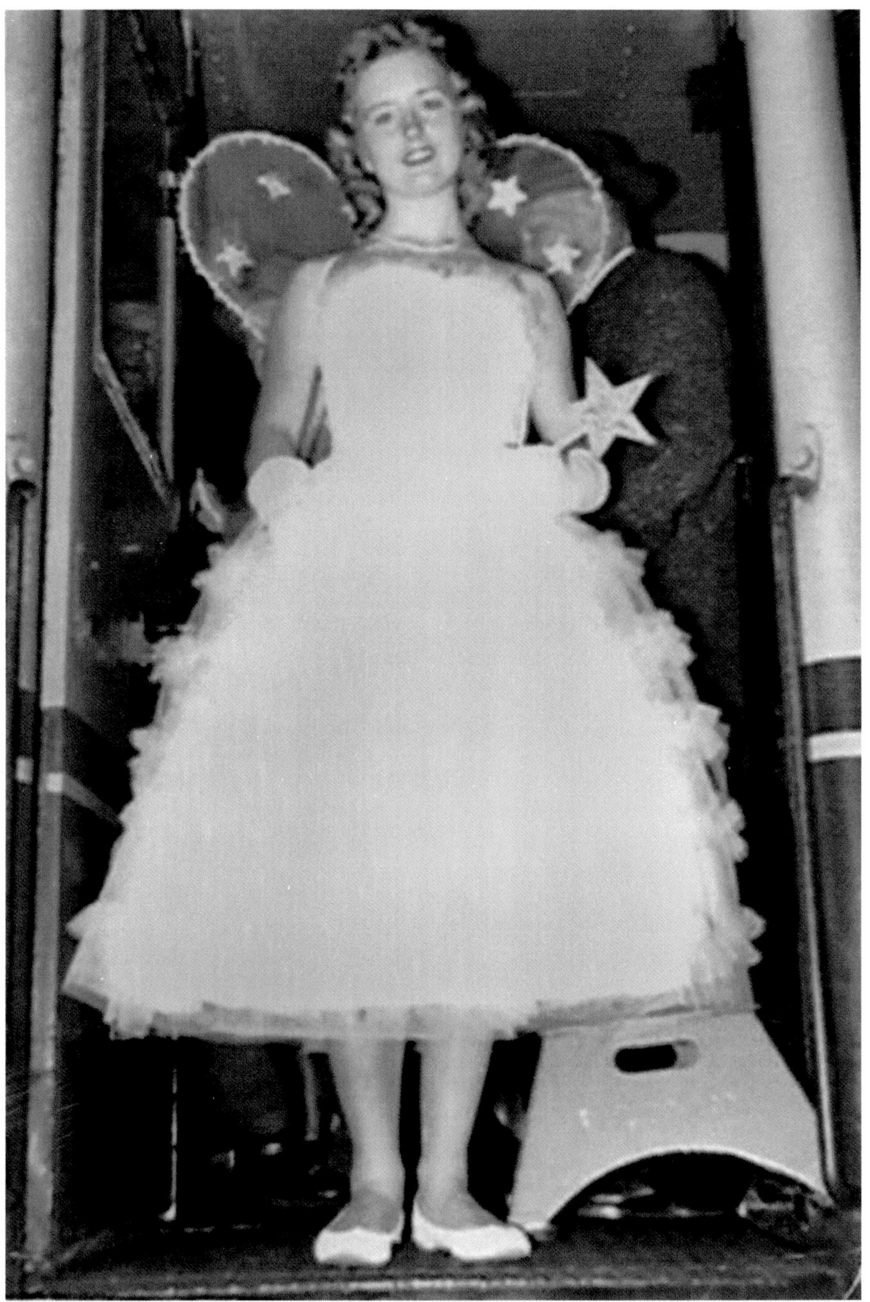

Fairy Princess Mary Anna Tignor Sylvia on the Cox Santa Special, 1957. *With permission of Mary Anna Tignor Sylvia, courtesy Betty Carol Stevenson Private Collection.*

their older siblings, ended up on the shoulders of dad or in the arms of mom. They walked the short distance to their Ashland homes, or searched to find their automobiles, on which the moisture had begun its surrender to the chill of a cold December Virginia night, ultimately turning to frost.

Through the escaping steam vapor coming from beneath the old RF&P coach cars, which occluded their windows as they stood emptying their precious cargo, Gene Luck surveyed the surroundings. It was so different from what he had seen the previous two years. Then, he simply viewed an immense crowd of people—rich, poor, of all colors and walks of life—united in their desire to lift their young children for a glimpse of Santa Claus. Tonight though, he'd joined them; he was one of them. He watched them: a jovial old man in a red suit, high school kids in their band uniforms, young ladies in their prom dresses and children in their Sunday best. There were even grown men in clown suits—receiving nothing in exchange but the satisfaction of knowing that they had helped their neighbors and total strangers experience the joy of the season. For one moment, an entire town knew nothing but camaraderie—a singleness of purpose. They had shared a common desire to forget all the cares and concerns of the world around them for just one night to see the world through the eyes of their children. What a wonderful experience.

As the red rear-end marker lamps faded from view, Joe and Jacqueline Andrews and Fairfax Davis turned and walked toward Cox Incorporated. For almost one hundred years, it had been a part of Ashland. They knew that the town's residents saw it as more than a place where goods could be purchased. To the best of their ability, they had attempted to return to their town some of the joy they felt in being there.

A year later to the day, December 6—this time, a bright and sunny Saturday afternoon—the Cox Santa Special ran again. Sadly, it would be its final journey. Oh, the crowds would come. The children would delight. The beautiful high school girls in their prom gowns, tiaras, wings and magic wands would charm the socks off the high school boys in the brass band that played "Santa Claus Is Coming to Town" before the grand entrance of Santa Bob Jeffers. However, little more than a year later, in 1960, Cox Incorporated would shutter its doors for the last time, unable to compete with marketing forces it could not control.

Fifty-three years later, at the mere mention of the Santa Claus Train, the people of Ashland not only recall the 1955–58 legacy of the Cox Santa Specials in incredible detail and with great delight but will also

come see santa
AT
Cox's
In Ashland, Va.
Every
Saturday Morning
FROM
10 to 12 noon until
Christmas
Come in and talk
with Him
— AND —
Have Your Picture
Taken If Desired
We would like to thank you, the general public for making our first "Cox's Santa Special" a great success. The response was so heartwarming we plan to make this our annual affair.
Thanks Again - - - -
COX'S

Cox Incorporated advertisement, "Come See Santa," 1957. *From* Herald-Progress *image, courtesy McGraw-Page Library, Randolph-Macon College.*

remind you—in case you didn't know—that their Santa Train was the first Santa Train.

Sometimes, it's at a table inside the Iron Horse Restaurant with newcomers or visitors who are fascinated by the sculpted tin ceiling tiles. Other times, it's diners who are seated outside beneath the awning who are in awe of the antebellum mansions, meticulously kept in a rainbow of colors. Then, there are those who simply pause momentarily from their hobby of photographing trains that pass right through the center of town. At some point, someone inevitably will pipe up and comment, "You know, this place looks as though it might have been some kind of store or something." Just as the server begins to set down a refreshing glass of sweet iced tea for her guests, a train roars past, rattling the large display window. The lights on the lowering crossing gates flash and the clanging warning bells act as an impromptu metronome for the player at the keyboard of the restaurant's baby grand. The host, a longtime resident of Ashland, waits for the moment at which the roar and vibration subside to respond to their curiosity. With an endearing smile, she nods at her friends and proudly affirms, "Indeed it was. It was some kind of store."

CHAPTER 7

THREE GUYS AND A TRAIN

The skyline of Richmond is shaped more by its citizens' affinity for church steeples than for the number of its skyscrapers. In a city where codes tend to overwhelmingly discourage tall buildings and in which zoning regulations cluster structures according to their use, it's not unusual to find pockets of spires symbolically and physically dominating entire neighborhoods.

Prominent Richmonders also are as conscious of their religious affiliations as they are of their country club memberships, to the degree that on Sundays, it would almost be possible to stand at a single intersection and hold there impromptu sessions of local governing bodies or board meetings for some of its most prestigious businesses. The same hands that pass the offering plate during morning worship services are often shaken at the conclusion of financial transactions during the week.

Newcomers—mostly those hailing from points north of the Mason-Dixon line—sometimes complain that Richmond has always had a propensity for cronyism and exclusion. Considering that people tend to bond with those with whom they share common interests or heritage, it's likely a fairly valid assertion, although no more common here than anywhere else.

At the east end of Monument Avenue—a fabled thoroughfare sporting a luscious green median, wide enough to accommodate touch football games or Easter egg hunts—stands a northward-facing equestrian statue of Confederate general J.E.B. Stuart. Stuart Circle, a traffic rotary at the center of a busy Richmond intersection, is bounded by a former hospital-turned-condo, a large apartment building and several houses of worship. Within a block or two are a dozen more churches and a synagogue that houses one of America's oldest Jewish congregations.

The steep curved steps of the First English Lutheran Church allow its parishioners an unobstructed view of ol' Jeb Stuart as they exit the sanctuary. Facing north, as a fallen hero, forever guarding the south, he's but a block from an even larger traffic circle with a black wrought-iron fence surrounding an even more imposing statue—that of southward-facing General Robert E. Lee.

Gene Luck allowed few things to preclude his attendance at First English Lutheran. While the railroad operates day and night, seven days a week, fifty-two weeks out of the year, aside from instances of extreme emergency that might demand their attention, railroad executives usually are immune from being disturbed on Saturdays, Sundays and holidays. They're afforded the privilege of having that time regularly reserved for themselves and their families.

The son of a railroad clerk, Luck's family relocated to Richmond from his birthplace of Selma, Alabama, and, most likely due to their friendly outgoing nature, immediately fit right into the social fabric of the city. He and his brother, Bob, both graduated from John Marshall High School, named for the fourth chief justice of the United States—a man regarded as the most influential American never to have been elected president. Since Richmond had but two high schools—the other named for another Virginia statesman, author of the Declaration of Independence Thomas Jefferson—the Luck boys got to know everyone. Gene was figuratively on the inside track.

The pews of First English Lutheran could boast of several other prominent Richmonders, including well-known names in local entertainment. Harvey Hudson, a north side boy, was barely out of his teens when he became a familiar voice on WRVA radio. Later a morning fixture at WLEE, he dated starlets and rubbed elbows with the toasts of Broadway and Hollywood, songwriter Bernie Wayne, Frank Sinatra and Milton Berle among them.

Another was legendary Charlie Wakefield. Few people could coax emotion out of a keyboard as ably as he did. Wakefield was a fixture at Richmond restaurants and clubs, as well as on local radio, for most of his life. What most people found amazing was that Charlie Wakefield was blind.

Paul Pearce, Charlie Wakefield's stepson, came from a family of musicians. Pearce's mother, Katherine Waymack, was a talented singer. Both she and Wakefield were products of Richmond's Church Hill neighborhood and performed together in dance bands. "After their respective spouses passed away, Mom and Charlie married," Pearce said. "She would accompany him to all of his appearances, including the Miller & Rhoads Tea Room and the Santa Trains—which he especially enjoyed."[36]

In tandem with celebrated theater organist Eddie Weaver, the two would perform at the Tea Room to the delight of diners as they set the musical stage for models on the fashion runway of the store's downtown Richmond flagship location. As a youth, former Miller & Rhoads employee Fred Dill, while waiting to visit Santa in the Tea Room, was introduced to Wakefield by Dill's mother, explaining that they were cousins. Young Fred was a bit startled when Wakefield asked the boy to come closer, in order for the blind musician to feel the features of his face. After a few seconds, Charlie smiled, nodded his head and said, "You look like your father."[37]

A book could (and should) be written about Charlie Wakefield because of his musical ability—not his physical disability. There was no sheet music to guide him. What people heard came from the heart, because what he played was all in his head.

Wakefield could play the accordion, whose portability made it an ideal instrument for train travel. When a young evangelist named Billy Graham scheduled some of his hugely popular crusades in East Coast cities in the 1950s, the RF&P operated chartered trains allowing the faithful to attend them. Wakefield was enlisted by his friend and fellow parishioner Gene Luck to accompany the trains' passengers in the singing of hymns while en route.

Another member of the church was a carpenter at Miller & Rhoads, Arthur Hood. "Chuck," as he was known, knew every square foot of the huge store. He was constantly taking the elevator from floor to floor to help create displays or make repairs. Typical of the family nature of Miller & Rhoads, Hood's father-in-law, George H. Mason, a company carpenter, was instrumental in his being hired in 1945.[38]

When Miller & Rhoads made the decision in the early 1950s to remain open later during the holiday shopping season, it was decided to hire a second Santa for the extended nighttime hours. Hood, whose size and build generally mirrored that of Santa William Strother, applied for the job. Having helped build and assemble the set each year, he knew the routine well. With Strother's aid in applying his makeup and donning the fur-trimmed costume and leather boots, Hood made the managers at Miller & Rhoads feel satisfied that they'd found the perfect candidate. Santa Chuck fulfilled his role for thirty-five years.

It was fortunate for the store, because when Bill Strother and his wife returned to Hollywood in early 1957—where he'd been an actor and stuntman prior to the couple's early 1930s move to Virginia to open a bed-and-breakfast in Petersburg—they were involved, as passengers, in a tragic automobile accident. Bill Strother, the ingenious man who created and copyrighted the Miller & Rhoads "Real Santa" concept, died. His wife survived but never fully recovered from her injuries.

Oddly enough, to help fill the void and to accommodate the demand for the duties of the increasingly popular Santa, Miller & Rhoads called on the talents of a 1942 John Marshall High School graduate named Hansford Rowe. Hansford distinguished himself for many years in local theater and would go on to become a celebrated character actor on the New York stage and in network television productions. Eventually, Rowe moved to Los Angeles and there landed supporting roles, becoming a very familiar face in movies and on television. When Hansford Rowe left Miller & Rhoads, Dan Rowe, his brother, took his place, and in 2013, he remains a "Legendary Santa," at the Children's Museum of Richmond.

Possibly over a potluck supper some Wednesday evening in 1957 at First English Lutheran Church, the three friends—Gene Luck, Chuck Hood and Charlie Wakefield—might have gathered and the Cox department store Santa promotion may have come up in conversation. The three, after all, represented the essential elements of the idea: trains, entertainment and Santa Claus. Fifty-six years later, no one knows exactly what transpired to pique Miller & Rhoads' interest in sponsoring a Santa Train from Richmond's Broad Street Station over the RF&P Railroad. We know only that it was able to sustain operating its own special trains until 1971, when the RF&P no longer provided passenger service, and its successor, the National Railroad Passenger Corporation (Amtrak), lacked the resources to grant the store's request to continue the tradition.

In the ensuing fifty-six years since the first Santa Train left the station, as was the case at Cox Incorporated, the decision-makers have long since passed on, taking with them their expertise in and their specific knowledge of their respective store's marketing plans. Although the end came thirty years later, in 1990, Miller & Rhoads suffered the same fate as Cox. Likewise, the detailed records of neither retailer's specific plans with regard to initiating the Santa Trains are available, so we've relied on interviews, phone calls and research provided by former co-workers, friends, family members and railroad data.

Charlie Wakefield was already an experienced RF&P traveler, having served as a musician aboard a number of excursions at Luck's request.

Having just begun to don the Miller & Rhoads Santa suit in the afternoons and at night, no doubt Chuck Hood found the discussion interesting.

Gene Luck had already worked with the owners of Ashland's hometown retailer, Cox Incorporated, coordinating the arrival of Santa Claus on a regularly scheduled RF&P passenger train to mark the beginning of the 1955 and 1956 Christmas seasons. Now, in 1957, he had again collaborated with the Cox people, this time to operate a special train that would bring Santa to Ashland. Instead of merely stepping off the train and walking across the street to the store, a special RF&P train would whisk them through the night on a nonstop journey to Richmond and back, riding the same train Santa had taken from the "North Pole."

Based on advanced ticket sales and the need to double the size of the train to accommodate demand, Luck was convinced that, like his other RF&P special trains (the Caboose Train, Redskins Specials and Theater Excursions), the Santa Claus Train was going to be a successful promotion for Cox and would certainly garner favorable publicity for the RF&P Railroad. With the comparatively meager resources available in the Cox Incorporated promotional budget and the relatively small retail draw of mostly rural Hanover County, one annual train was all the store and the town of Ashland could reasonably support.

The same did not apply to Miller & Rhoads in Richmond, though.

In 1956, Richmond's population—at over 200,000—was one hundred times that of Ashland. Additionally, downtown locations were opened in Roanoke, Lynchburg and Charlottesville. Tidewater Virginia was ripe for Miller & Rhoads to enter. The store's management was even looking at eventual expansion into the Carolinas and Tennessee.[39]

Luck also had to consider that his resurrection of twenty old coach cars, while efficient, wasn't cost free. Suppose the same equipment could be scheduled to operate Santa Specials for communities in cities at other points along the RF&P. Possibly one of the department store chains in Northern Virginia would be interested—maybe Fredericksburg as well. Instead of their wheels rusting away in the weeds behind Broad Street Station, those twenty surplus 500-series coach cars could be busy burnishing the rails from one end of the RF&P to the other.

Luck sat down at his office with a calendar and formulated a plan to present to the marketing department at Miller & Rhoads. Since he'd already begun using the same equipment for the Washington Redskins football specials, it wouldn't be available on Sundays. Besides the fact that equipment wouldn't be available, in 1957 Virginia, proper families didn't even allow their children to attend movies on that day. No merchant would risk being affiliated with an event that promoted the secular aspect of Christmas on the Sabbath. A majority of the population steadfastly supported the commonwealth's Sunday closing laws—blue laws, as they were called.

If he proposed scheduling the train for a Sunday, how would Gene Luck be able to darken the doors of the First English Lutheran Church on Sunday? Sure, the Redskins football specials ran on Sundays. The club's owner gladly advanced him all the tickets he wanted in order to sell rail fares from Richmond to Washington, but who cared? Back then, the Redskins didn't have a prayer—on Sunday, or any other day.

CHAPTER 8

OK, HERE'S THE PLAN

To call Gene Luck creative was a gross understatement. He could most likely have held his own in a compelling conversation with Thomas Edison, Alexander Graham Bell or Rube Goldberg. The man had an imagination based in practicality and intuitiveness that could boggle the mind.

In the 1940s and early 1950s, prior to his tenure with the RF&P, Luck was a traveling sales manager for the Wortendyke Manufacturing Company (later, Camp Manufacturing Company, a maker of paper grocery bags). He scorched the two-lane highways and dusty back roads of the Southeast in a 1937 Buick. One of his sons, Bob, pointed to his father as the inventor of automobile air conditioning, although the name Gene Luck won't be found on any document in the U.S. Patent Office in that regard.

"Back in those days, Dad would head for the Carolinas in the summer heat and humidity in that old Buick. He'd be sweating to beat the band. One day, an idea hit him as he passed a business that sold ice. Dad stopped the car, went in, bought a two-hundred-pound block of ice, put it in the floor of the back seat, rolled up the windows and poked a small hole in the floor to let the water drain out," the younger Luck chuckled. "As the ice melted, the inside of the car would cool. My mother, my brother—Bucky—and I always said Dad was the first to invent AC in an automobile."[40]

Bob Luck also hinted at the possibility that his dad might have had a hand in social change. "In addition to all the fun excursions that Dad was responsible for initiating, one really interesting trip was the Caboose Train. It was initially billed as being a father-son outing," Luck recalled from his home in Franklin, Virginia. "But it later became a mother-daughter event as well. Finally, it was billed as being fun for the entire family." In a world where young girls were more or less expected to fret away their spare hours rearranging the furniture in their doll houses or accompanying their mothers on shopping trips, Gene Luck saw everyone as a potential patron of the Richmond, Fredericksburg & Potomac Railroad.

No doubt, the executives in the marketing department of Miller & Rhoads were both curious and anxious to meet the man who had helped create such a splash of publicity for the small Cox department store in Ashland. Based on the reports they'd seen and heard, they might have felt that Gene Luck was going to propose that Miller & Rhoads' real Santa board one of the RF&P's passenger trains at some point north of town and make his grand entrance into Richmond at Broad Street Station.

Because the Cox store was ideally located, directly on the railroad tracks, and the platform of the Ashland depot was but a few steps from the store's front entrance, it was a unique setup that made all the sense in the world. Miller & Rhoads, unfortunately, stood some twenty blocks east of the big domed station that served Richmond. Logistically, this simply wouldn't work unless Luck intended to propose a parade or motorcade down Broad Street to the store. Retail competitor Thalhimers already had an illuminated extravaganza that covered the same exact route at night, ceremoniously delivering Santa to its downtown location. Doing a parade might simply be seen as Miller & Rhoads' attempt to imitate its rival's annual feat. There was no need to do that; Miller & Rhoads already had a much more successful marketing plan. It had the real Santa. He parked his sleigh and eight tiny reindeer on the roof of the store and came down a chimney into the seventh-floor Old Dominion Room, an auditorium and large meeting room that at Christmastime was converted into a stunning scene of winter wonder: Santaland. Whatever Luck might propose would have to substantially enhance the copyrighted program the store already had in place. If it ain't broke, don't fix it.

There was an air of anticipation and curiosity, if not a possible hint of skepticism, as the RF&P Railroad's director of passenger services was ushered into a meeting room in the seventh-floor business office suite, high atop the sales floors of Miller & Rhoads' flagship store. No one questioned his credentials. Luck was no stranger to the Richmond business community. He'd had a long and illustrious career with Wortendyke, rising from the ranks as a stenographer to become vice-president, having enterprisingly engineered its sale to Camp Manufacturing. He was no naïve babe in the woods when it came to sales promotion. That was well known.

Affable but business-like, Gene Luck was introduced to those in attendance. Formalities dispensed with, Luck began to outline his plan to operate not one, but two Santa Claus Trains on Saturday, December 7, that would depart Broad Street Station. At Ashland, the train, loaded with giddy tots and their parents, would stop to allow the boarding of the Miller & Rhoads Santa, along with his Snow Queen. The train would then proceed farther north to the railroad junction town of Doswell, where the Santa Special would stop once again. Here, while Santa continued through the train, stopping to speak with each child, the locomotives that had pulled it would be uncoupled from the north end of the train. Mostly unnoticed by the passengers, the locomotives would then be operated to the other end of the twenty-two-car Santa Special on a parallel siding and be reattached to the opposite end. Within a few moments, the train would ease southward and pick up speed for a nonstop run back to Broad Street Station.

Santa and his Snow Queen would immediately begin walking through the train from its rear car upon boarding at Ashland. They would continue through until reaching the other end, stopping to chat with each child along the way. Only the train itself would be reversing direction at Doswell—Santa and party would continue right on through the cars, reaching the rear car at some point before the train arrived in Richmond. Care would be taken to ensure that Santa's entourage had adequate time to socialize, even if it meant slowing the train down to accomplish this. Once stopped at the station, Santa and the Snow Queen, using a motorized cart, would be whisked upstairs to Broad Street Station's main waiting room—as if by magic. The exciting affair would culminate when the passengers from the train would join Santa, who would light the huge, enchanting tree in a brief but rousing round of Christmas favorites accompanied by an organist. If his duties at the M&R Tea Room and at Loew's Theatre would permit, it possibly could be Eddie Weaver, who played the organ for Santa for the event. The stage would then be literally set for Santa to invite all of the children to join him downtown at Miller & Rhoads, to dine in the Tea Room and visit him at Santaland. At that point, a limo would be waiting to take Santa and the Snow Queen back to Ashland to await the next train of enthusiastic greeters.

Luck went on to add that in order to obtain tickets for any of the trains, parents would have to make a visit to Miller & Rhoads. None would be sold by the RF&P.

And what would all of these children be doing until Santa appeared on the train? After all, anyone traveling with a small child, whether on a train or

Miller & Rhoads
VIRGINIA'S FINEST DEPARTMENT STORES

SANTA CLAUS TRAIN

1183

on the R.F.&P. Railroad

Leaves Broad Street Station – 4:30 P.M.

SATURDAY, DECEMBER 5, 1964

75¢ each – No Refunds or Exchanges

The RF&P/Miller & Rhoads Richmond Santa Train tickets could be purchased by passengers only at the downtown store, 1964. *Lewis Parks Private Collection.*

in the family car, knew that little ones tended to have short attention spans and were prone to temper tantrums.

Santa has elves at the North Pole to help him, so it would only be natural for him to have his elves on the train. They could hand out candy canes, spread Christmas cheer and lead each car's occupants in chanting seasonal songs in anticipation of Saint Nick's appearance in their car.

The grand entrance would begin with musician Charlie Wakefield, who would precede the Snow Queen and Santa throughout the train. Gene Luck seemed to have thought of just about everything.

What about Cox?

There was really no conflict. It served a clientele in a town of roughly two thousand people, twenty miles north of Richmond. Its train would have been operated the night before. It had its own Santa. The Miller & Rhoads Santa and Snow Queen would be seated discretely in a limousine at College Street, north of the station, on the opposite side of the tracks until the arrival of the train.

There must have been some head scratching and surprised expressions on the faces of the Miller & Rhoads executives when Gene Luck concluded his presentation. Apparently you can teach an old dog new tricks. They'd of course have to look at the budgetary side of the proposed Santa Train, but quite possibly, the passenger service director of the RF&P had given them a vehicle (no pun intended) with which to broaden the appeal and heighten the exposure of the store's real Santa Claus. This was sure to generate a wave of very positive public relations for Miller & Rhoads.

More than likely, they were thinking, "Thank heavens Gene Luck hadn't decided to approach Thalhimers, first."

CHAPTER 9

IT'S GOING TO BE A GREAT DAY

The Richmond, Fredericksburg & Potomac Railroad, while relatively short in length, has always been an extremely busy one. Its strategic location has resulted in it being called the "richest little railroad in the world." Stories of layoffs were almost unheard of, while its history of hiring every member of entire families is legendary. Temple Blunt of Ashland, a retired conductor, for example, was a fourth-generation railroader and a proud third-generation RF&P employee.

Frequent and well-attended company picnics resembled family reunions. The monthly company employee publication, the *Rail-O-Gram*, included anniversaries, birthdays, births and passings. If your son or daughter graduated from high school or received a college degree, everyone knew about it. The RF&P made every effort to see that each employee was at home for Christmas, even if this resulted in permitting freight train crews arriving at Potomac Yard in Alexandria on Christmas Eve to quickly detatch their locomotives, couple up to their caboose car at the opposite end of their train and travel quickly back to Acca Yard in Richmond with no other freight cars in tow.

Understandably, in 1957, when the company sent out the call to its employees for volunteers to staff the Richmond to Ashland Miller & Rhoads Santa Train (as well as the Cox Incorporated Santa Special), it was blessed with an overflow of assistance. The railroad and its employees took great pride in their community. As the tickets for the Cox special and the two Miller & Rhoads trains quickly sold out, there was no doubt that their

Miller & Rhoads
ALL ABOARD!
Get Your Tickets Now for Rides on the M&R
SANTA TRAIN
Take a thrilling and exciting ride on a real RF&P train with Santa Claus himself aboard.
That's right, a real train ride with Santa himself aboard, along with a host of helpers—clowns, elves and the Snow Queen, too.
All trains will leave from the Broad Street Station on Saturday, December 5th and Saturday, December 12th. Four train rides each day at 9 a.m., 11:30 a.m., 2 p.m. and 4:30 p.m.
Everyone must have a ticket, no matter what the age. So don't delay because tickets will not be available at the train station. Purchase them in advance at Miller & Rhoads 1st Floor Ticket Booth Downtown only. Sorry, no mail or phone orders.
So get set for the train ride of the year on the Miller & Rhoads Santa Trains. Get your tickets tomorrow for 1.50 ea.

Miller & Rhoads Santa Train Richmond to Ashland newspaper advertisement, 1959. *Lewis Parks Private Collection.*

consists (the makeup of the train) would swell to the full twenty-two-car limit imposed by the availability of equipment.

Memos began flowing between every concerned department to ensure that all three moves would go flawlessly and reflect positively on the RF&P. There was to be at least one railroad employee in charge of every two cars from an hour before departure until after the very last passenger was on his or her way up the ramp into the station's waiting room upon the train's return. Doors were to be opened prior to boarding and closed before the train moved. No one was to be permitted to pass between cars while the train was in motion. This was to ensure that everyone who boarded with ten fingers and toes went home with none missing.

An order went out from the office of the trainmaster to the stationmaster at Broad Street Station and to the mechanical department, specifying that "twenty of the company's best 500-series coaches" would be assembled on Track Seven for each train. Additionally, two cleaned, fully fueled E8 diesel-electric locomotives were to be positioned back to back, coupled to the train, with all steam and air connections made and tested. It had been only five years since the

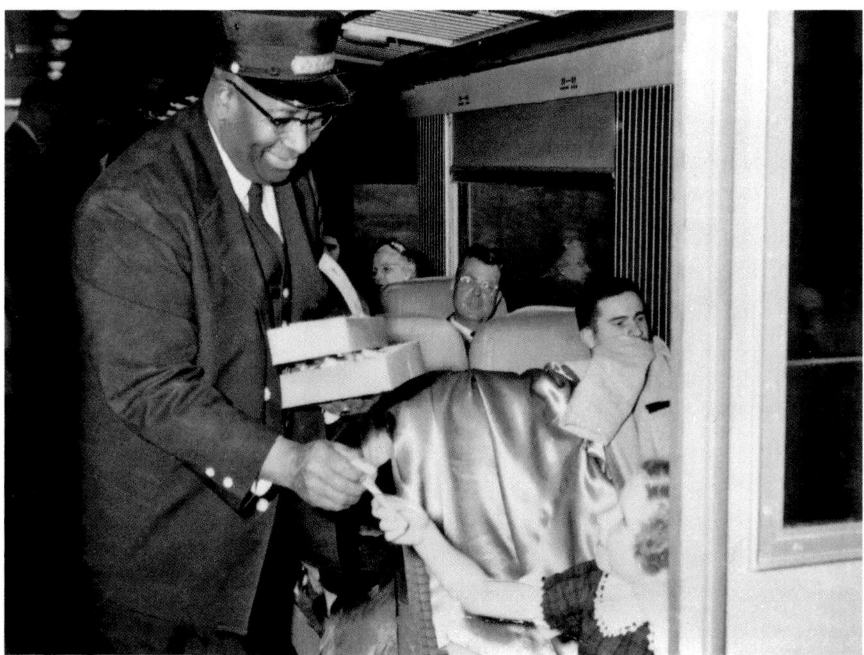

Sometimes even railroad employees became Santa's helpers. Here, Cheryl Wakefield Hamm receives candy from an RF&P crew member, 1957. *Cheryl Wakefield Hamm Private Collection.*

RF&P had operated its last steam locomotive. Its diesel locomotive fleet remained spotless outside and impeccably well maintained operationally—just as its steam locomotives had been lovingly cared for and well kept until the fire was dropped on the last one in 1953.

Before he went down to the platform to board the Cox Santa Special on Friday night, December 6, Gene Luck perused the train orders that would be given to the conductor and the engine crew who would operate it. He spoke with the train dispatcher in Richmond to make sure no detail had been overlooked. As a result, the train went flawlessly into the night, making friends of 2,300 passengers for the RF&P.

On Saturday afternoon, the same equipment stood ready to make two round trips on behalf of the Miller & Rhoads department store. The coach-cleaning staff had worked its magic overnight. Plastic wrappers that had found their way off cherry-flavored suckers were swept up—along with some of the suckers themselves that had found their way onto the floor. An overly excited tot had apparently accidentally soiled one of the seats, but its cushion had been replaced. Every window had been wiped clean of tiny fingerprints. Clean towels filled dispensers in the restrooms, cone-shaped paper drinking cups were once again in ample supply next to the water coolers and all trash receptacles had been emptied.

A sea of people overflowed the cavernous waiting room of Broad Street Station and spilled into the seemingly endless concourse on its way to the boarding gates. A gigantic decorated Christmas tree stood in the middle of the corridor where the concourse and the waiting room joined. It had yet to be lit. That was a rite reserved for the white-bearded visitor from the North Pole. All of this, of course, was in addition to the press of normal Saturday afternoon crowds, gathering in preparation to depart for destinations in the sunny southeast, like Miami, Jacksonville and Atlanta, or disbursing after having arrived from shivering origins along the Northeast corridor.

The muted roar of the crowd was suddenly broken by a few errant notes from the keyboard of a Baldwin organ that had been strategically placed near the large tree in order to provide Christmas music for the day's planned festivities. It was not the musician who was expected to play the instrument, however. Rather, a couple of technicians who were making sure that electricity was reaching it, while at the same time ascertaining that choruses of "Jingle Bells" and "Here Comes Santa Claus" would indeed flow from the two large wooden speakers to which it was connected. Once satisfied that their efforts would result in a joyous songfest, the workmen packed up their tools and hustled off to perform other duties.

From the wrought-iron walkways that connected the office towers on either side of the terminal's signature arched front-entrance window that faced out onto Broad Street, a jovial Gene Luck and a number of the excited Miller & Rhoads executives looked down into the station with a great deal of pleasure. While they could not visually determine which persons were there to accompany their children on the Santa Train or which ones were about to embark on a vacation to balmy Florida, the sight of so many people jamming the floor below indicated that a lot of folks were going somewhere.

The afternoon winter sun pierced through the rounded windows beneath the side of the dome that faced west, providing shade for the cashiers selling cigars and magazines at the newsstand that occupied the west wall of the large room. At the same time, though, the sun's positioning was nearly blinding the ticket agents behind the counter where they greeted passengers on the opposite side of the cavernous domed room. Heat escaped and rose toward the vaulted ceiling from the grates around which were built polished oak benches, worn smooth from over thirty-five years of travelers. Four abreast, they stretched across the spacious waiting room. More seating was

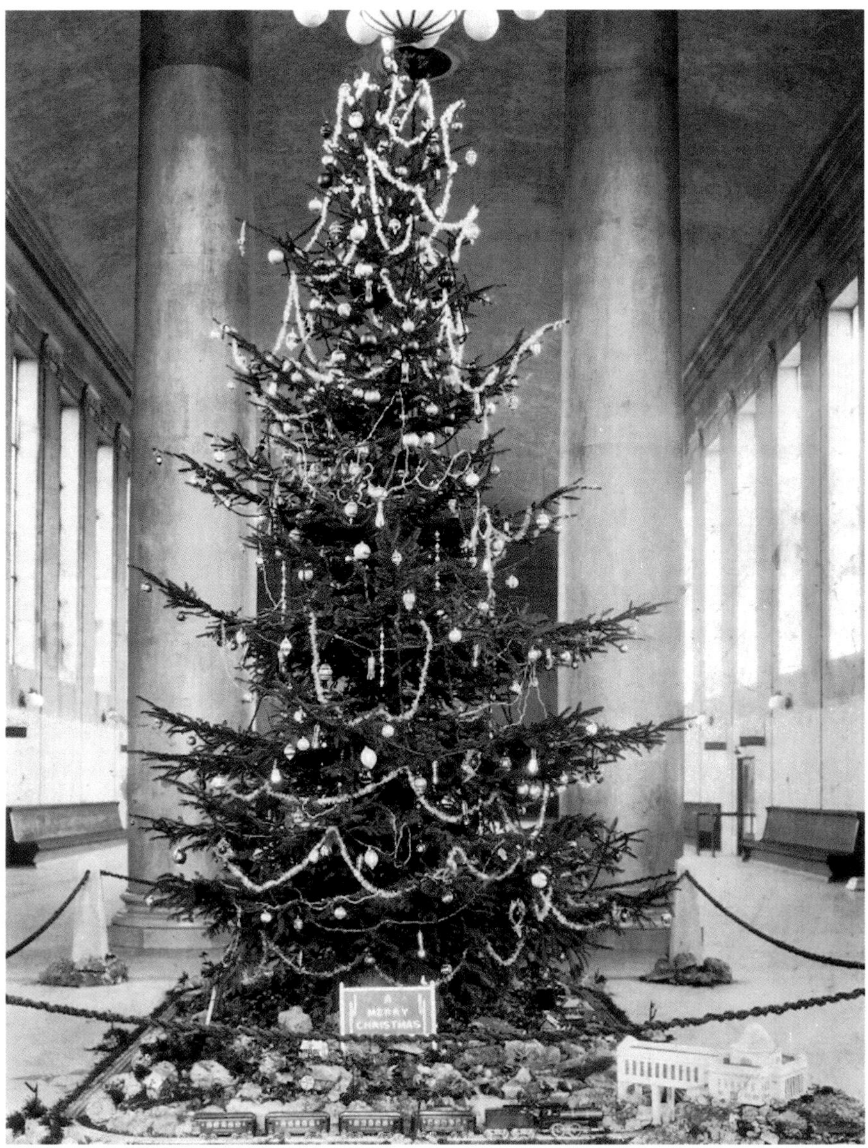

Broad Street Station Christmas tree, circa 1938. *Courtesy RF&P Railroad Historical Society.*

available in the long concourse, where tall, narrow windows didn't thwart the sunlight's attempt to supplement the output of the coal-fired heating plant, warming noted architect John Russell Pope's expansive transportation cathedral. Judging from the number of passengers who vacated the shadows to huddle in the better-lit portions of the station, the slowly disappearing sun was very much welcomed.

Bobbie Kay Wash and a friend brought their children for the trip: "We dressed my two boys and hers in Carter's outfits."[41]

There were few seats remaining down on the main floor. The curved driveway, through which private automobiles and taxicabs normally would have passed to drop off passengers, had been blocked off this afternoon and turned into an impromptu parking lot, in which hundreds of cars had been carefully wedged. It appeared that it would likely be necessary for some of them to occupy the well-kept grass plaza, which flowed like a leafy green carpet down to the sidewalks bordering the city's main thoroughfare.

Yes, this was going to be a great day.

For young Nancy Allen, her brother, John, and their sister, Barbara, this was going to be a great family outing with their dad, an architect for the C&O Railroad. They frequently parked next door at the Hot Shoppes, where car hops would deliver delicious grilled cheese sandwiches with big dill pickle spears and rich creamy milkshakes. They would then sit on the sloping hillside behind the restaurant to watch trains.

"No grilled cheese sandwiches on the afternoon of the Santa Train. We even had trouble finding a place to park. We were going to have our personal audience with Santa after we picked him up at the 'North Pole,'" Nancy remembered.[42]

"Now boarding on Track Number Seven, the Miller & Rhoads Santa Claus Train. All aboard, please." The announcement sounded like the voice speaking to Moses as he confronted the burning bush, resonating off the towering walls of the 196-foot-long concourse. Because his words had a natural tendency to echo, the station announcer had to deliver them clearly and in a slow and deliberate cadence. The uniformed gate usher, standing at attention beneath the iron sign identifying his station as the entranceway to the stairs leading down to the boarding platform, struggled for a second but overcame the resistance of the heavy wooden door. With a wail of excited, high-pitched shrieks, the mass of tots, toddlers and adults funneled toward a comparatively tiny pore in the big Indiana limestone wall. Within a matter of minutes, the entire chamber emptied, leaving one poor soul and his battered suitcase, sitting in comparative silence, waiting for an announcement regarding the departure of his train, an Atlantic Coast Line Railroad local that would stop at Weldon, North Carolina.

"My grandfather Dr. Guy R. Harrison took my hand and urged me to hold on tightly so we'd not get separated in the crowd," Ed Crews distinctly

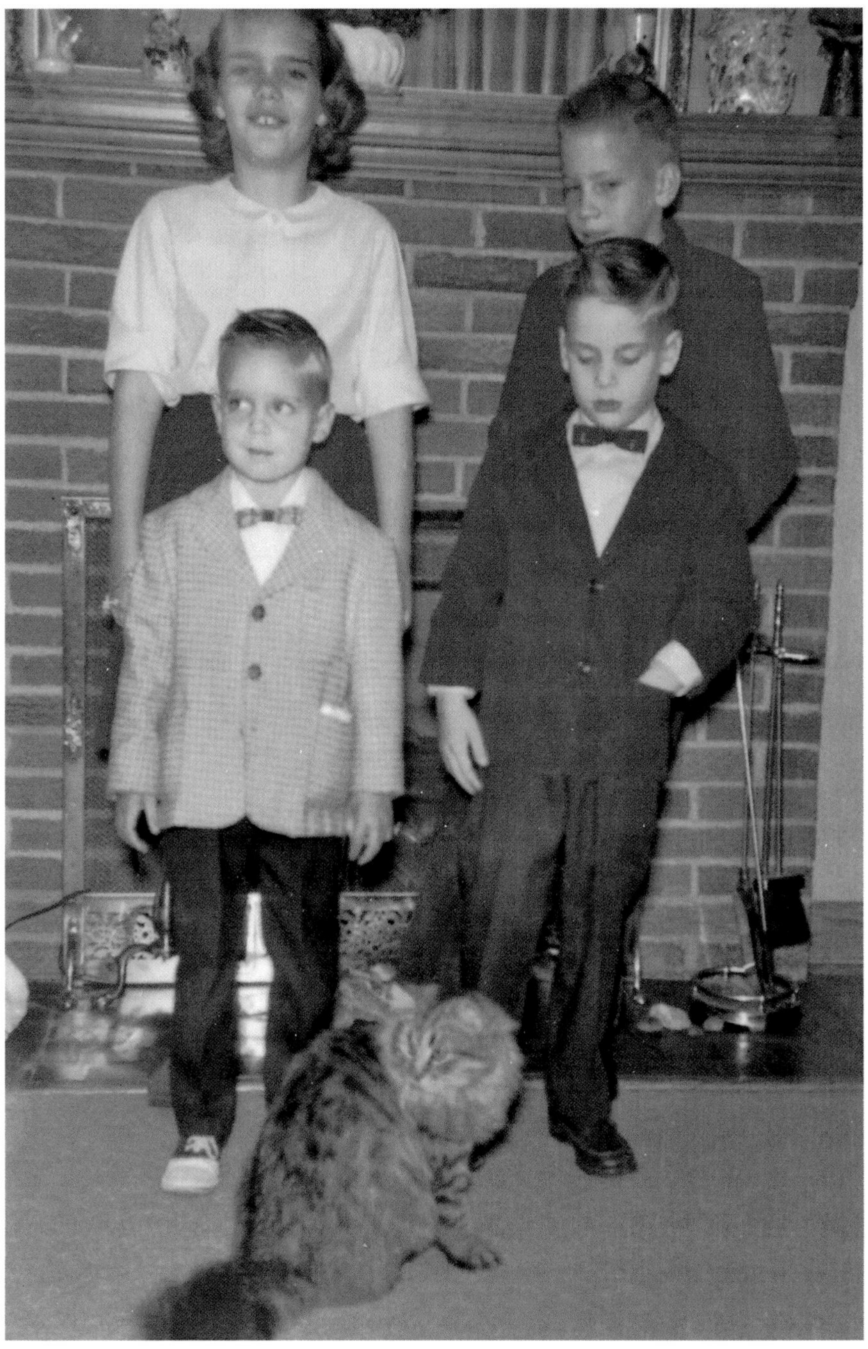

(Clockwise) Pam Spicer (Anderson), Wayne Peters, Chuck Akers and Ronnie Akers in their Sunday best for the 1963 Miller & Rhoads Richmond Santa Train. *Wayne Peters Private Collection.*

Broad Street Station parking lot in Richmond, Virginia, circa 1965. *Courtesy RF&P Railroad Historical Society.*

remembered. "He picked me up in his old 1937 car that he was still driving in 1960. We used to come to the station to watch trains. This time, I got to ride one."[43]

Down on the platform, at least one youngster had ignored the admonition of a Santa Train's car marshal not to run, for he suddenly and unexpectedly found himself on his hands and knees, a bit skinned up, save for the heavy winter coat and long pants he was wearing. As his face began to contort, he was about to break into tears. A young lady picked him up, comforted him and reminded him that he was about to meet Santa Claus. "You don't want him to see you crying, do you?" Shaking his head slightly with a sniffle that was soon daubed away with a tissue, the youngster and his mom stepped quickly aboard the blue and gray coach car, where the little boy began exploring the bright red cloth seats, his momentary tussle on the cold, hard concrete platform apparently forgotten.

After consulting his watch and getting a nod from stationmaster H.T. Anthony, the conductor of the first Miller & Rhoads Santa Train yelled out, "All aboard!" After scanning the boarding platform one last time, he raised and lowered his arm several times—a hand signal that meant, "Proceed." He then looked toward the locomotives, where the engineer leaned out of the cab window, his arm on the leather armrest, watching him. "Go north," ordered the conductor, stepping up on the vestibule and pulling twice on the cord above his head, confirming his directions and creating a shrill whistle twice in the locomotive cab. With a blast of compressed air released from the locomotive's control stand and the bell thumping as the afternoon shadows lengthened, the engineer advanced the throttle of the two big E8s, and the train eased into motion.

"My wife, Dare, and her friend Joann had taken our two daughters to ride the Santa Train, leaving me at home," Calvin Boles recalled. "The phone rang and my wife explained that she'd been in a minor accident. When I arrived in our other car, Dare told me to take the girls and go get on the train. When I got there, I took one under each arm and ran down the stairs, onto the platform as the train began moving. There was someone at the rear door who helped us get on. To this day, I don't know how we managed to get on that train!"[44]

John Bendall, the father of Nancy Bendall Emerson, Joan Bendall and John Bendall Jr., worked for the RF&P and served as a conductor on the Santa Train. Mrs. Emerson explained this fact to *The Polar Express* author, Chris Van Alsburg, at a local book signing once. Van Alsburg stopped for a moment, asked about the train and appeared fascinated. "I always told our boys whenever we read that book that Pop was the conductor on the Santa Train," said Emerson.[45]

It was the type of thing that families enjoyed, John Strother, brother of Donna Strother Deekens, recalled. "For us, it was a father-son outing, and it was especially a treat for Dad since he was raised in Ashland where the Santa Train was headed, even though I thought we were going to the North Pole!"[46]

Once the last car had cleared the curved track at the east end of Broad Street Station, the Santa Train began to pick up speed. A goodly number of the young children had never been aboard a train before, and as such, their natural tendency was to explore their alien surroundings. There were ashtrays built into the armrests of the seats to toy with; cone-shaped paper drinking cups that, when pulled, fell and scattered to the floor; and the door at the end of their car that magically slid open and shut with a hiss of air, each time someone approached it.

One curious tyke wandered up to the door just as it opened and suddenly was faced with an older man in an overcoat, wearing a brown Fedora that covered his graying head. Harold Heenan, a foreman at the RF&P's Acca Yard Shops, knelt down and eyeballed the small boy. "Where do you think you're going?" he asked with a smile.

RF&P conductor John Bendall served as a conductor on the Santa Train from Richmond, 1963. *Nancy Bendall Emerson, Joan Bendall and John Bendall Jr. Private Collection.*

The stunned youngster, unable to say anything, simply stared at Heenan, simultaneously widening his eyes and opening his mouth. "You know, Santa Claus is going to be coming along in a little while. He knows you're here to see him, but if you aren't at your seat, he might miss you. You wouldn't want that to happen, would you?"

The little fellow slowly shook his head from one side to the other in agreement. "Well, let's find your mom and pop and make sure you're in your seat when Santa gets here, OK?" The little head moved again, this time, bobbing up and down excitedly. The kind man grasped his hand and led him back to his anxious parents, who thanked the railroader for corralling their errant son. He tipped his hat, smiled and walked on toward the end of the car to make sure everything else was in working order for this special excursion to the North Pole.

"My sister, Lori, and I rode the Santa Train with my grandparents one year—my first train ride," fondly remembered Graham Wilson. "We were told we were going to the North Pole. It snowed once, as I recall, and as we pulled into Ashland, there was Santa and the Snow Queen, standing there on a stage of white. I loved the experience of Santa greeting us in the smaller space of the train car," he added, "as it was as if he came to see us instead of us going to see him in Santaland at the store. We enjoyed both kinds of visits of course, but for me, the train ride was an extra thrill!"[47]

Parked at the corner of College Street and Railroad Avenue, on the east side of the RF&P tracks in Ashland, a long black Miller & Rhoads limousine sat, its motor running to keep its occupants warm and its exhaust curling upward into the fast-fading sunlight of a late December Saturday afternoon. Santa and his Snow Queen chatted as they peered southward for signs of a northbound train's headlight. Their task was made a bit more difficult because the town was all aglow from the strings of multicolored holiday lights that hung across the streets from utility poles. The electrically lighted candles and wreaths in the windows of homes and businesses made the little town appear like one of the storybook villages that grace the fronts of Christmas cards.

A block away, on the other side of the tracks, business was brisk at Cox Incorporated. The previous night, its Santa Special had arrived in Ashland, and according to reports on radio and in the morning paper, over two thousand people had ridden. Cox's Santa was inside the small department store from 10:00 a.m. to noon and 1:00 p.m. to 3:00 p.m., greeting children and posing for pictures. Looking at his watch, it dawned on the Miller & Rhoads Santa that his country cousin had likely just concluded his day and was probably headed off to the rooftop to "feed his reindeer." This was the explanation that he used to excuse himself when the last tot had wandered off the stage of Santaland at the big store downtown.

For a second, Santa stopped and contemplated the festive scene all around them. "You know," said Santa, in an exclusive interview with us at his summertime workshop, "the snow was beautiful, but especially beautiful in Ashland some years."[48] How tragic that the man who had originated the concept of the real Santa would not be present to board Miller & Rhoads' first Santa Train. Tragically, Santa Bill Strother had lost his life in an auto accident earlier that year. This talented man would surely be missed at the time of year when he was the star of the show. Help had been brought in to see that the legend continued to live, but a big hole had been left in the tightknit M&R family.

The gentleman who sat opposite the Snow Queen in the limo had just begun donning the famous red suit only a couple years earlier to assist Strother when the store extended its holiday hours. Santa began enjoying his evening meal in the Tea Room before a round of nighttime visits from young Richmond children, whose mothers and fathers opted to do some Christmas shopping during the time when the pace at the big store on Broad Street was a little less hurried.

For attractive, blond Miller & Rhoads Tea Room runway "Missy Model" Sue Ferrell, being called upon to serve as a Snow Queen was an infrequent but not unusual assignment. "Sue was one of the best-ever M&R models," commented Carol Bryson, who coordinated the fashion shows at the Miller & Rhoads Tea Room at the time.[49] Like the RF&P Railroad, there was a camaraderie among Miller & Rhoads employees, an unspoken desire to do just about anything that was asked when the store needed assistance, especially when a new program or marketing venture was being launched.

"Because the Charlottesville store didn't have its own Santa, he and I were asked to be there on Friday night once from 6:00 p.m. to 9:00 p.m. Trouble was, we had to be at the Richmond store at about 6:00 a.m. Saturday to get into costume for the Santa Train," Sue Ferrell said. "That was a long day."

She'd helped the jolly ol' elf perform his magic in Santaland on more than one occasion, so she didn't mind being asked to perform the Snow Queen role walking through a moving train, crammed to the rafters with bug-eyed little boys and adoring little girls.

"I was once pulled over and ticketed for speeding on my way to the store to get dressed for the Santa Train," Sue Ferrell laughed. "I told the police officer I was the Snow Queen and Santa was waiting for me to ride the Santa Train. He just looked at me and said 'Sure.' I got there at the last minute before we had to head for Ashland. Santa never said a word."

One of the first, if not the first, Santa Train Snow Queens, Ms. Ferrell recalled that the M&R "Matron Model" Frances Cox, affectionately known as "Mama Cox," who lived in Ashland (and was part of the Cox department store legacy), used to invite her and Santa over to dine on pasta at her home when they were working the night train.[50]

Just as that thought crossed her mind, the limousine driver, who was patiently waiting with her and Santa, announced the appearance of a distant headlight.

The train—all twenty cars—slowed down and pulled past them so that they could board the door at the very rear. Then, they would begin their

The Miller & Rhoads Santa and Snow Queen Sue Ferrell wave to returning Santa Train passengers at Broad Street Station, 1959. *Courtesy Valentine Richmond History Center.*

long walk to the opposite end of the Santa Train. They would be preceded by a familiar talent, Charlie Wakefield, who sometimes sat at the piano at the Tea Room, joining accompanying organist Eddie Weaver, who charmed the audience and often zinged models with his razor-sharp wit. Wakefield would enter each car playing "Santa Claus Is Coming to Town"—their cue to come through the door to touch the heads and hearts of each child in attendance.

Wakefield also played other seasonal favorites. "To this day, every Christmas," remembered Ed Crews, "I think about it [the Santa Train], especially when I hear the song "White Christmas."[51]

Nancy Allen, now Nancy Allen Perrow, recalled her excitement when on her nineteenth birthday at a Forest Hill restaurant, she recognized the man playing the piano and singing: "It was Charlie Wakefield, from the Santa Train."[52]

Although the train would be rocking and rolling, those aboard the train were assured that it would be at a speed that would allow them to move about relatively safely. It was also explained that the train's conductor

Celebrated organist Eddie Weaver performs dressed as a locomotive engineer at Richmond's Loew's Theatre WurliTzer, circa 1956. *Jody Weaver Yuhase Private Collection.*

would confer with Santa to make sure that the train would not arrive into Broad Street Station until Saint Nick and the Snow Queen had seen every child, even if that meant that the train would reduce its speed and crawl along through the Acca Freight Yard before reaching the end of the line, around the bend at Broad Street Station. There would be a point, at Doswell, where the train would be stopped for about fifteen minutes before reversing directions to return to Richmond, but the Santa party would continue in the same direction, going car by car and seat to seat for almost two hours. Then, with just a few moments to compose themselves and grab a bite to eat, the two would hop back into the limousine for a quick return trip to Ashland for an encore performance. Later that evening, there would be another train, one also filled with holiday revelers of all ages, waiting to welcome them to town.

The limo's doors opened as the red lights flashed; the bells began to clang and the crossing gates lowered into position to halt motorists in approaching automobiles. The two special guests stepped out into the chilly air and walked to the highest point at which College Street and the rails of the RF&P met. There, they stood back away from the approaching train and began waving as the diesels slowed down, allowing escaping steam to envelope the front end of the lead locomotive, exaggerating the glow of its headlight as it slowed to a creep.

Both the engineer and the fireman stuck their heads out the cab window and door to get a gander at what Santa brought them. They smiled widely and waved wildly at the Snow Queen. She winked, smiled and waved back. They also acknowledged the presence of Santa. (Grown men, you see, may have differing perspectives when it comes to Santa Claus, but very few of them will argue about the striking appearance of a beautiful young woman dressed in a gown.)

"My dad, Charles Curley Jr., a member of the Old Dominion Chapter of the National Railway Historical Society, rode the rear car, which was leased by the RF&P for the train," laughed Charles Curley III. "It was cold, and when Dad boarded the Snow Queen at Ashland, he gave her a warm embrace. Santa looked at Dad and said, 'Find your own Snow Queen; this one's mine.' They laughed, and Santa continued with his duties."

The younger Curley, given the opportunity, opted to ride the train's engines. He noted, "Santa was great, but I love trains."[53]

The spotless windows with which the train left Richmond soon were covered by small fingerprints, as all the children in each car rushed to the east side of the tracks for a glimpse of their hero and the Snow Queen. Seeing so much activity, yet hearing not a sound, it almost reminded one of being present for the showing of a silent movie. It didn't take a lip reader to interpret the words that were being screamed from the mouths of the children as they gathered at the windows and began jumping up and down on the seat cushions.

Bill Barnett, whose father, E.E. Barnett, was a brakeman on the RF&P, sometimes accompanied his dad on weekends when the elder Barnett worked the local freight. One snowy Saturday morning, the younger Barnett recalled, "after leaving Richmond, we had to stop in Ashland and set off some cars. Our train was backed into the siding to clear the main line for a passenger train that was coming. I was then told that it was the Santa Train and that Santa was getting on here at Ashland. There was a very light snow falling. As the train arrived, it looked like it was full of rabbits. Every window had several little noses pressed against the glass as the children were all looking for the first sight of Santa and the Snow Queen. It looked like it could have been a Norman Rockwell Painting."[54]

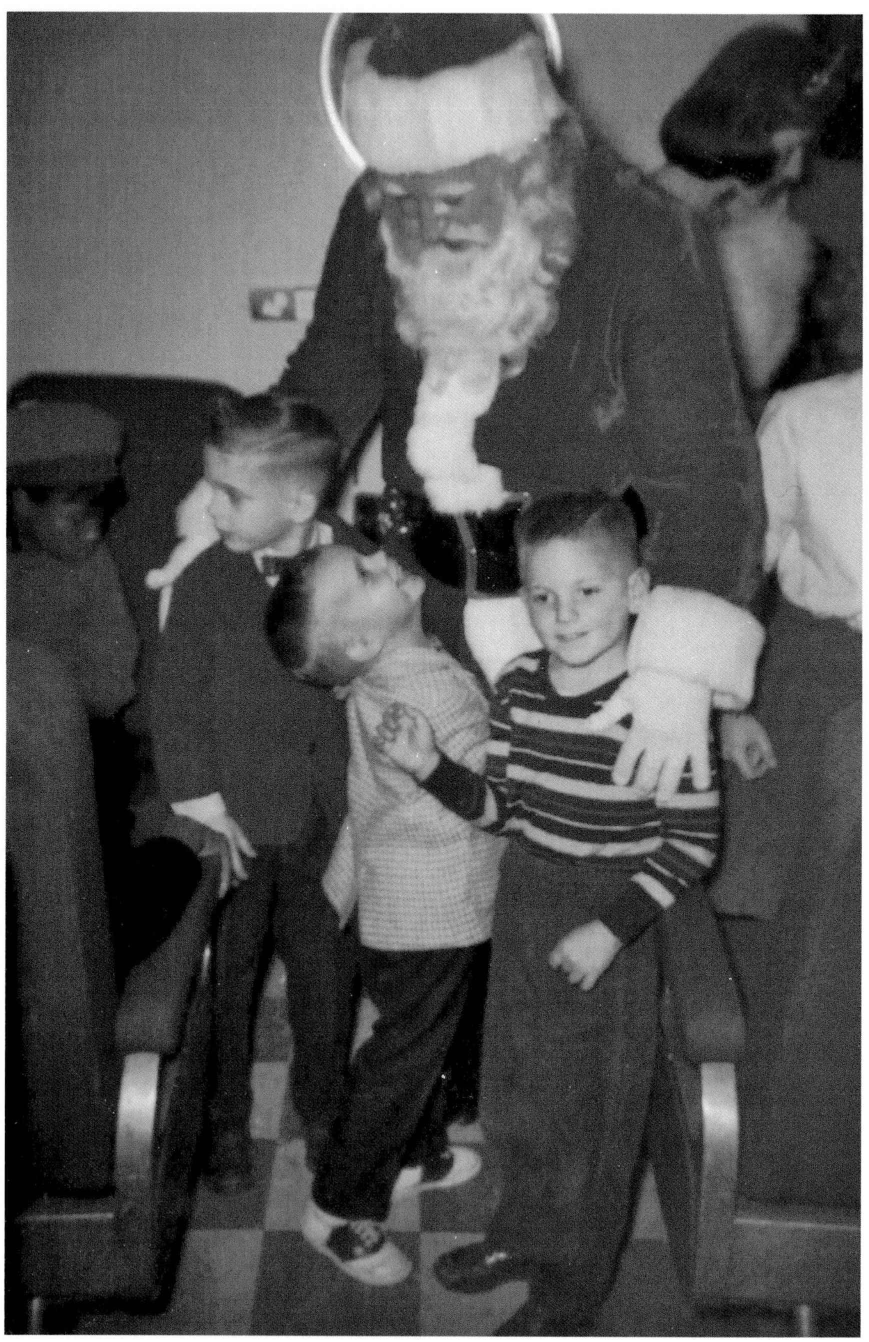

From left to right: Ronnie Akers, Chuck Akers and Mark Anderson enthusiastically greet Santa aboard the 1963 Miller & Rhoads Richmond Train. *Wayne Peters Private Collection.*

Santa and the Snow Queen board the Santa Train sponsored by RF&P and Miller & Rhoads in Ashland, Virginia, 1969. *Charles Curley III Private Collection.*

"Santa Claus! There he is!" was surely on the lips of all the children on the Santa Train.

With a thud, the rear vestibule door of the last coach of the Miller & Rhoads Santa Train opened. The train's conductor occupied the bottom step, now barely moving. He leaned outward and began waving his white Kerosene lantern horizontally in a signal to the engineer to stop as he approached the celebrities he was about to board. To the sound of the brakes taking hold of the round steel wheels as they squealed and went dead silent as the train came to a halt, he took a handful of white paper towels and with them began wiping down the hand rails. This was a customary ritual, an attempt to remove as much road grime from them as possible before Santa's white gloves and the Snow Queen's beautiful dress could become soiled. He reached back into the coach and grasped a metal stool, placing it on the pavement to enable the pair to step more easily up into the vestibule of the coach, observing carefully to see that the skirting of the Snow Queen's dress did not become entangled on anything that might tear it.

With everyone ready, the RF&P conductor lifted and lowered his lantern, vertically this time, warning everyone nearby that the train was about to proceed, and then followed Santa aboard the train. Two toots sent from the conductor were followed by two loud blasts that resonated in the locomotive cab, as the Santa Train silently moved north. A few people noticed that Shirt Blanton, occupying his wheelchair on the west side of the tracks, was waving his flashlight at them as they left town. Others watched as Randolph-Macon College began to move past their windows. Most people, however, had their eyes fixed on the aisle, looking back toward the rear of the Santa Claus Train, waiting excitedly for the man of the hour—Santa Claus, accompanied by his beautiful Snow Queen.

The brightly clad clowns, who had entertained everyone at the station, roamed the length of the train, among them, Barnum & Bailey's famous "Felix." There were balloons that were twisted amazingly into the shapes of animals or contorted into the form of funny hats and colorful crowns. An army of Santa's helpers, including Terry Mitchell, from local high schools handed out coloring books. Mitchell was a rare male member of the Miller & Rhoads Teen Board representing Highland Springs.[55] Mary

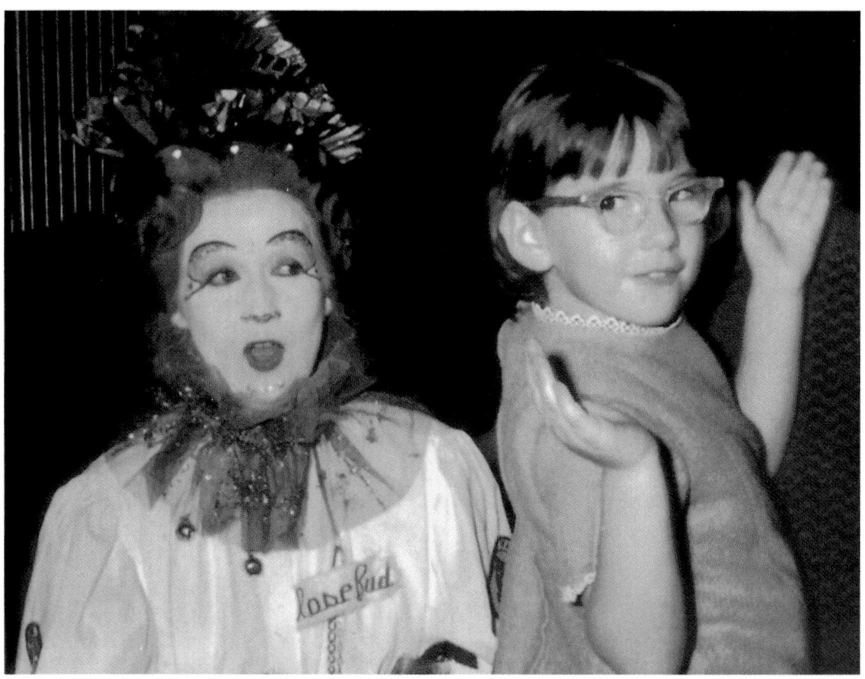

Rosebud the Clown and Melodie Heath Warren share a light moment aboard the RF&P/Miller & Rhoads Santa Train, 1969. *Ed Heath Private Collection.*

Louise Stewart Johnson became a Snow Queen after learning about the position while a member of the Teen Board and worked many Santa Trains between 1965 and 1968. Others distributed candy canes to the outstretched hands of youngsters, the smiles of whom had obviously been visited by another nocturnal houseguest—the tooth fairy. Quickly, the candies were unwrapped, and just as quickly, they began to turn lips a rosy shade of red.

Ed Crews, whose grandfather was an oral surgeon, remembers receiving a candy cane as a treat. "My grandfather wouldn't let me eat it right away. There was no foolishness [like] eating candy before dinner, and under no circumstances did he want me to suck on it," he chuckled.[56]

"I was so shy at age fifteen that my aunt, Mary Valentine, who was a Miller & Rhoads' employee in charge of the second floor, insisted that I ride the train as one of Santa's helpers, so she called up the promotion manager and made the arrangements," admitted Judith Valentine Frayser. "I discovered I had a voice." She remembered leading the singing of the children and parents in her train car. "I never thought of the Santa Train being a character-building experience, but it was."[57]

Every now and then, an excited clown or giddy Santa helper would come streaking through the cars yelling out, "Santa is only three cars away; Santa is only two cars away!" As the number of cars decreased, the excitement and anticipation increased, until finally, the door at the end of

Richmond musician Charlie Wakefield leads the singing before Santa's coach's arrival on the RF&P/Miller & Rhoads excursion, circa 1969. *William E. Griffin Private Collection.*

the car opened, the music from Charlie Wakefield's accordion began to swell and a familiar bearded face appeared: Santa Claus!

For young Cheryl Wakefield Hamm, who was a helper aboard the train in 1966, this was doubly exciting because she was the daughter of musician Charlie Wakefield. "About the time my dad came through, playing 'Santa Claus Is Coming to Town' on his accordion, that was the signal that Santa was following close behind, and indeed, he and the Snow Queen would show up to greet every child and parent."[58]

But instead of an outburst of screams, a hush gripped those who spied him first and spread throughout the length of the car, like the silence of the surf gently withdrawing back across ocean sands after the thunderous crash of a giant wave upon a beach. It was a show of reverence usually reserved for royalty. But then, after all, this was the real Santa Claus.

"Santa would touch every child on the head," remembered Jean Howe Duke. "It was so exciting for my boys, Gary and Billy, and I know we rode it for at least three years in the mid-1960s."[59]

His red velvet hat was trimmed in white. His flowing snow-white beard was set off by a complexion dominated by rosy cheeks. His knee-high, black leather boots matched his wide, brass-accented black leather belt. He quietly bent over to speak to the first child he saw, patted her head and spoke with a soft voice that immediately calmed her as she leapt forward to hug him. He listened intently as she described the specific doll she wanted, the type of cookstove she dreamed of and the vacuum cleaner she hoped Santa would leave under her tree when he visited her family's home on Christmas Eve. And yes, he'd love to have milk and cookies (chocolate chip being his favorite) waiting for him when he came down the chimney. With a wink to mom and dad, he said he'd heard that she'd been an exceptionally good girl this year, so he'd be checking his list to make sure she had lots of toys and goodies to look forward to on Christmas morning.

"While I had no problem granting the wishes of most young boys and girls, some requests tugged at dear ol' Santa's heart strings," Saint Nick confided to us at his summer workshop, as a tear welled up in his eye and found its way down his rosy red cheek. His soft familiar voice quivered for a second, as he continued. "There were those who asked for things like the return of a father who was away, serving his country. And then, there'd be the little girl who would simply ask Santa to make her grandmother well again."[60]

The Miller & Rhoads Santa and Snow Queen greet passengers, including Harriet Heath (left), aboard the Richmond to Ashland excursion, 1969. *Ed Heath Private Collection.*

Santa greets admirers on the RF&P/Miller & Rhoads Santa Train, as RF&P's Gene Luck (background) looks on, circa 1969. *William E. Griffin Private Collection.*

Miller & Rhoads Santa greets sisters Melodie Heath Warren and Celeste Heath holding cousin Tammy Subotich on the train, 1970. *Ed Heath Private Collection.*

Even so, thinking back on it, Santa recalled, "Loving all these experiences, and enjoying talking to all the kids and parents, I would say, this has been the best Christmas present I ever received."[61]

As soon as the Santa Train pulled into the siding at Doswell and stopped, an army of Gene Luck's RF&P elves pounced on the connections that fed air and steam from the locomotives back into the train. Since it was cold, it was vitally important that the chore of moving the engines to the other end of the train for its return to Richmond be made as quickly as possible, to restore the flow of heat and air for passenger comfort. Hardly a soul aboard the train likely noticed. The joy of the moment undoubtedly distracted the Santa Train's passengers as the two long diesel locomotives slipped past them. They probably didn't even feel the slight nudge as the locomotives were coupled to the same car that Santa and the Snow Queen had initially boarded. The white-bearded gentleman and the attractive young lady were almost halfway through the train, having greeted about eight hundred boys and girls and their moms and dads. And just as quietly, as the sun began to hide behind some orange-tinted clouds in the western sky of Hanover County, the now southbound Miller & Rhoads Santa Train

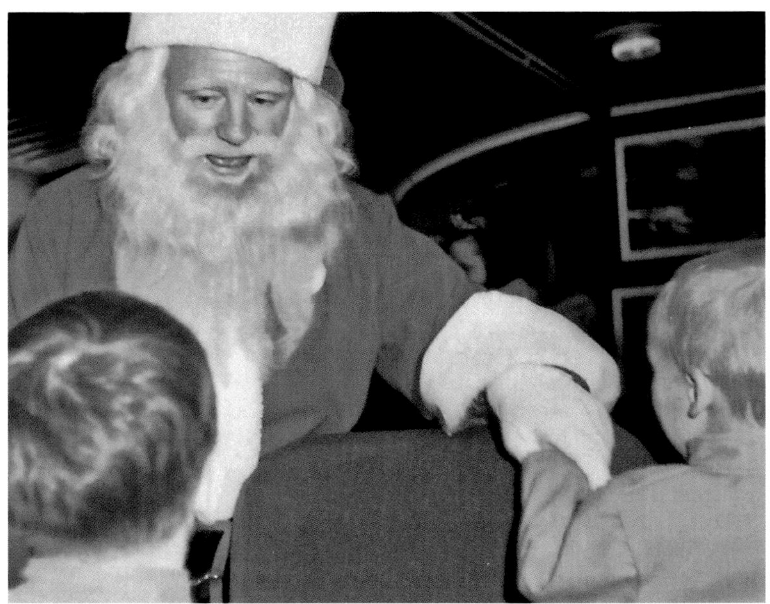

An excited Wes and Mark Nuckols meet Santa aboard the 1969 Richmond Miller & Rhoads Santa Train. *Santa Charlie Private Collection.*

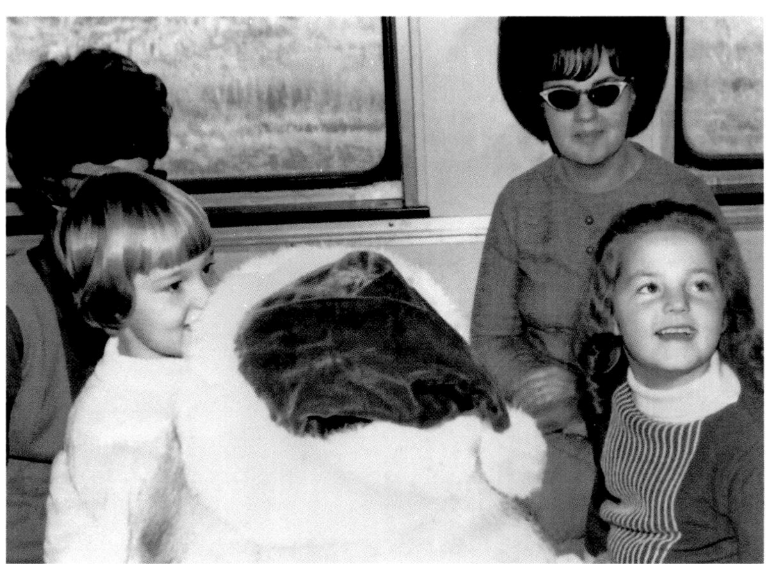

Santa (center) and (left to right) Jean Roberts, Wendy Loscomb Morton, Charlotte Loscomb and Kim Loscomb Vickers on the Richmond train, 1969. *Morton and Vickers Private Collection, in memory of Charlotte Loscomb.*

quickened its pace as the combination of red and green signal lights ahead brought thoughts of the time of the season to the engineer and his fireman in their locomotive cab.

Every now and then, the engineer would look back along the side of the train for a lantern signal from the conductor, cautioning him to slow down or urging him to speed up. Their instructions were for Santa Claus himself to determine the pace of this train.

"Our family and friends always took the evening Santa Train," Charles Nuckols said, "so we could see the lighting coming on as we approached the city returning to town." It was a special treat for him and his wife, Nancy, as well as their two children—Wes, age seven, and Mark, age four. "We always went in a big group. Prior to Santa arriving in our car, we'd be entertained by Charlie Wakefield on his accordion and 'Whitley the clown.'"

But for Nuckols, the most impressive sight was at the end of the trip, as everyone was leaving Broad Street Station: "There stood Santa on a platform, with a sign saying, 'Come visit me at Miller & Rhoads'—looking like 'Man Mountain.' He had a commanding presence."[62] (Charlie Nuckols himself became a Miller & Rhoads Santa Claus in 1980. He continues to occupy the chair as a real Santa every holiday season.)

Darkness began its dominance of the sky as the green lights at the north end of Acca Yard began to flicker. As the Santa Train inched toward the narrow, crooked Westwood Avenue Bridge that spanned the big railroad yard, the conductor's lantern was sighted, bobbing up and down rapidly, indicating that all Santa business had been concluded. It was now OK to make the big turn, past the FFV (Famous Foods of Virginia) cookie bakery and head into the same track at Broad Street Station from which they had departed just two hours earlier. The lights inside the station lit up the city skyline to the east. The lights of the tall downtown office buildings formed their own festive backdrop to the terminal building. The nose of the lead engine was eased up to the white sign, placed there by the stationmaster, noting the proper spot at which to halt the Santa Special so that each door on every car in the train, when opened, would allow the occupants to step onto the concrete platform.

A white golf cart sporting the circular emblem containing a triangle that formed the logo of the RF&P Railroad was at the extreme west end of the boarding area. It had very important guests to meet. Santa and his Snow Queen had to be in place to begin the singing of Christmas favorites and

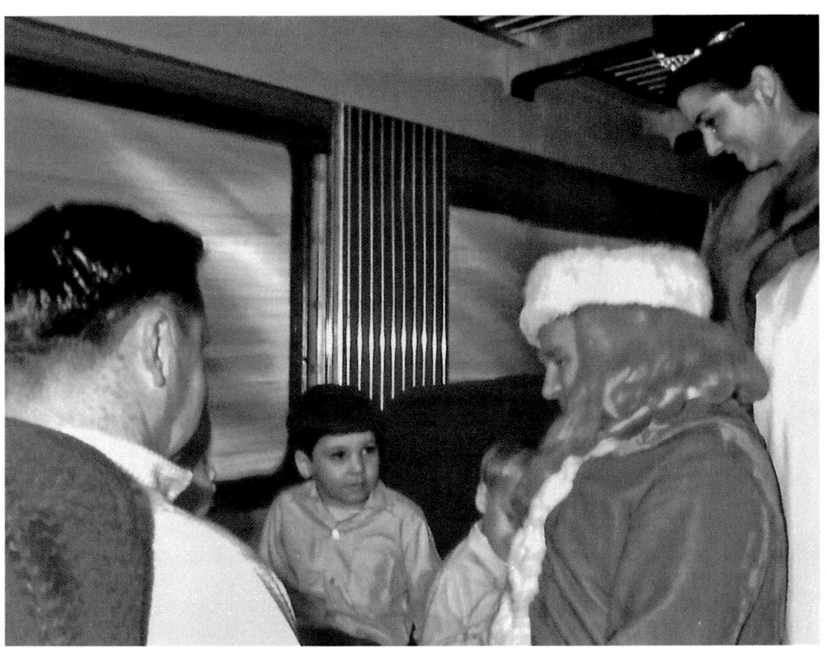

The Miller & Rhoads Santa and Snow Queen talk with brothers Wes (left) and Mark Nuckols en route back to Richmond from Ashland, 1969. *Santa Charlie Private Collection.*

The Miller & Rhoads Santa and Snow Queen wave goodbye at Broad Street Station, following the Richmond to Ashland Santa Train run, 1963. *William E. Griffin Private Collection.*

to light the majestic tree that seemed to reach the very top of the domed waiting room ceiling.

The procession of little folks and adults moved a bit slower ascending the ramps leading up to the station's interior. The sandman also was waiting to keep an appointment with the same children, who had awoken in the morning full of excitement with the prospect of seeing Santa and riding the train with him. Magically, Saint Nick and the Snow Queen were on a platform at the top of the ramps, waving to them and urging everyone to gather around the tree. The huge expanse of the big train station gave the small electric organ the courage to mimic the mighty Wurlitzer pipe organ Eddie Weaver played at Loew's Theatre across the street from the downtown Miller & Rhoads store.

To the cheers of everyone in the station—visitors, patrons and passengers—who had arrived on the Santa Train, the great fir tree erupted into myriad colors, set off by glittering aluminum icicles and bright ornaments of all sizes and colors. It was truly breathtaking.

Santa stepped forward, thanked everyone for riding with him on his triumphant arrival into Richmond and urged them to come see him at the Miller & Rhoads downtown store. He would be there every day the doors were open until Christmas. As the crowd roared its approval, Santa and the Snow Queen wished everyone a good evening and slipped out the side entrance. Families with small children—some on dad's shoulders, others in baby carriages—made their way toward their cars or to the red and cream buses that plied Broad Street, stopping in front of the station on their way throughout town.

"So, are you ready for Christmas?" asked young Nancy Allen's father as her family exited the station.

"You bet, Daddy," she recounted the scene from years ago. "But you know what would be good right now—one of those grilled cheese sandwiches and a great big milkshake!"[63]

For the Miller & Rhoads Santa and the Snow Queen, however, it was a quick bite to eat in the backseat of the speeding limo as they headed back to Ashland to await the nighttime run of the Santa Train. Ladies with their hair up in bandanas and men in baseball caps were already aboard the twenty cars of the Santa Train in Track Seven. They had only about thirty minutes to give it a quick change, collect every scrap of trash, clean the windows, replace the paper towels and drink cups and once again make sure that Santa's sleigh—the RF&P Santa Train—shone glossy and bright.

Gene Luck grabbed a quick sandwich and a cup of coffee from Julian's Restaurant across the street from the station. As he walked back across the darkened plaza in front of the big terminal, he looked up with a great deal of satisfaction. He'd kept his promise to former RF&P president Tom Rice (who had been named president of the much larger Atlantic Coast Line Railroad earlier in the year). He was filling trains with sports fans, theater patrons and businessmen. Now, he had demonstrated that it was possible to fill entire trains with children and their families—introducing them to the enjoyment of rail passenger travel. And quite possibly, he'd help create a holiday tradition.

But there was no time to think about that now. At 6:00 p.m., another twenty-car train of excited youngsters would be taking a train ride to the North Pole. He was probably as excited as the boys and girls waiting to see Santa.

Gene Luck was on a roll.

CHAPTER 10
ON A ROLL

The 1957 Richmond, Fredericksburg & Potomac Railroad annual report extolled the innovations overseen by its director of passenger service Gene Luck. His theater trains to New York and Washington received a standing ovation and demands for encores from enthusiastic patrons of the arts. Over nine hundred theatergoers boarded a special RF&P train to travel the short thirteen miles to Ashland employing vintage coaches and caboose cars for a night of entertainment on the lawn of the Barksdale Theater. An old diner was stripped of its table and chairs to make room for a chapel car, complete with organ, to transport the faithful to Madison Square Garden for a Billy Graham Crusade event. This gesture received national broadcast and press coverage. Gene Luck was giving everyone a reason to ride an RF&P train.

Of course, the report went on to mention the first Santa Trains, carrying 6,600 children and adults—one from Ashland, sponsored by Cox department store, and two that originated at Broad Street Station, featuring the Miller & Rhoads Santa. They were an immediate and resounding hit.[64]

While the Miller & Rhoads promotion grew and expanded with each succeeding year, however, the Santa Special operated by Cox Incorporated the following Christmas season, 1958, would be its last. Even though the Ashland retailer had endured everything from fire to the Great Depression, it could not fight progress. Despite its loyal patronage, no doubt due in great measure to the store's dedication to the community it had served for nearly one hundred years, it could not compete with the glitz, glitter and glamour

Miller & Rhoads logo sign from the Richmond, Virginia downtown storefront, circa 1989. *Donna Strother Deekens Private Collection.*

available in downtown Richmond or at the area's two new suburban shopping centers.

The Cox department store ads in the December 1959 *Herald-Progress* did not mention a Santa Special, but the paper did report news that construction had begun on twenty-two miles of Interstate 95, which would bring Richmond even closer to Ashland's doorstep. When Cox Incorporated finally closed its doors in 1960, plans were already in the offing for an even newer enclosed shopping mall in neighboring Henrico County. This one would be only ten miles away via Route 1.

In 1958, Miller & Rhoads was a thriving entity, however. It was engaged in a game of retail chess with rival Thalhimers. Miller & Rhoads had stores in downtown Roanoke, Lynchburg and Charlottesville and was considering expanding with additional locations in each major Virginia city.

Very much pleased with the results of the Santa Claus Trains it had operated over the RF&P in December 1957, the Miller & Rhoads executives examined maps that featured railroads serving their stores in the western part of the commonwealth to see if it would be feasible to expand the Santa Train promotion to any of them. Realizing that their expertise was in retail—not transportation—a call was made to the man who had brought them good fortune during the prior Christmas season, Gene Luck.

Their early spring 1958 meeting must have been in stark contrast to their conference the year before, when it was Luck who had requested an appointment with the Miller & Rhoads people. This time, he was appearing at their request. Before accepting the foreman's invitation to take the next car up, the old railroad man checked his watch against the iconic Miller & Rhoads clock. Generations of Richmonders, visiting the downtown store, when in doubt, always told their party to meet them under the clock. It wasn't a standard railroad clock, but for his purposes this day, it would do just fine. He was expected in the executive offices on the seventh floor in ten minutes. He was equally pleased that despite Richmond's worsening morning rush hour traffic, he had time to spare. The crowds were exacerbated by a first wave of diehard shoppers, who jammed the entrance to the store daily, especially on sales days—as if by being the first inside, the Dali Llama was going to confide in them the secret to happiness.

As the polished brass elevator sped upward, he tried to anticipate the reason for the meeting. He'd learned that for competitive reasons, the revelation of the details of any upcoming sales promotion campaign was strictly *verboten*. Gene Luck's thought was that it was far too early in the year to simply set up schedules for the Santa Trains for the upcoming Christmas season.

The sudden deceleration gave Luck a momentary feeling of near weightlessness as the car stopped just a couple of inches short of the floor. The smartly clad operator toyed slightly with the control handle, tapping it once or twice, and the elevator car's floor was suddenly perfectly matched to the office suite's. The operator reached across the opening, pulled back the polished-brass safety grate and announced, "Seventh floor, executive offices, Old Dominion Room. Watch your step, please." Luck smiled, nodded and thanked the young man, who was standing at attention, as if someone were going to appear, grab the handle and give it the white-glove test.

"Right on time," the lady who greeted him said with a very warm and inviting smile. "You are a railroad man after all, aren't you, and the trains must run on time, right?"

Luck could hardly hold back his laughter at the patronizing pun. "We aim to please," he responded.

After accepting the offer of a cup of coffee, he was shown into a meeting room as a couple of the other attendees arrived. He recognized one gentleman from working on the Santa Train who introduced him to the other. He was the manager of Miller & Rhoads' Roanoke store. The RF&P didn't come anywhere near Roanoke. They had only one branch—a short few miles of railroad connecting their main line just north of Fredericksburg with the U.S. Navy's Dahlgren Proving Grounds. Declared surplus following the war, the RF&P had acquired it, thinking it might prove to be attractive for industrial development.

A secretary with a steno pad and pencil, who Luck correctly assumed would be taking notes, closed the door behind three other gentlemen. Indeed, Miller & Rhoads was delighted with the activity that was generated by the Santa Trains. The executives were the first to admit to being quite surprised at the swiftness with which the tickets had sold out for both scheduled trains. The gentleman who was in charge of the meeting—an executive in charge of sales promotion—couldn't get over the amount of coverage they had received in the morning *Richmond Times-Dispatch*, as well as its afternoon twin, the *News-Leader*. The success of the trains had been duly noted over the airwaves of Richmond's radio stations, and the folks at Channel 6 had made mention of it on the televised evening news.

"We want to assure you that our promotional plans for the coming Christmas shopping season include a renewal of the Santa Train promotion. It goes without saying. We also want to explore the possibility of sponsoring a Santa Claus train that would benefit our store in Roanoke and, if it succeeds, nearby Lynchburg," the executive likely said. Before Luck could respond, the gentleman would have continued, "We realize we would have to arrange for the operation with a railroad that is serving that area. The Chesapeake & Ohio and Southern Railways both serve Charlottesville as well as Lynchburg, where we have stores, but neither operates through Roanoke. The Norfolk & Western Railway [N&W] serves both. While you can't speak for them, I'm sure, we felt that you might have connections with them that might permit us to find out if they would be receptive to a business arrangement similar to the one we've established with the RF&P."

Responding to their observations, Luck would have explained that the N&W in fact operated trains into Broad Street Station that forwarded through sleeping cars between Norfolk and New York, as well as a number of daily "short" trains, ferrying local residents between Richmond and Petersburg. He would have affirmed to the Miller & Rhoads managers that he would be glad to make inquiries on the store's behalf. "Confidentially, of course," the sales promotion executive would have emphasized.

"Of course," Gene Luck would have assured them.

As he drove back toward Broad Street Station, Luck thought about the N&W. It was a very pro-passenger and community-conscious railroad. So much so that, unlike its coal-hauling rival, C&O, N&W had generally spurned efforts by the makers of diesel-electric locomotives to get the railroad to purchase any of them.

Miller & Rhoads Santa Claus in Richmond prepares to meet little admirers, circa 1962. *Marilyn Hood Gunn, Carolyn Hood Drudge and Robin Hood Private Collection.*

The N&W's massive Roanoke shops did everything imaginable, including building and maintaining the line's fleet of coal-burning steam locomotives. The railroad felt that it would be offensive to its customers—coal producers—to couple up hoppers loaded with their product to a locomotive powered by an internal combustion engine. It feared the possible backlash by unionized miners if it showed any weakness in its ardent support for coal. To that end, the N&W had invested millions of dollars to research new ways to power its trains with modern coal-burning locomotives that would make it competitive with the cost effectiveness of diesels.

The N&W's steam engines were setting new records daily for speed and availability, but it still could not beat the "off the shelf" advantage—the

Miller & Rhoads Santa points toward the North Pole, holding Mary Mitchell Amos, while brothers Paul and Timothy Mitchell look on, circa 1962. *Paul Mitchell, Tim Mitchell and Mary Mitchell Amos Private Collection.*

standardization that came part and parcel with diesel locomotive ownership. You could order them from a catalogue, painted to your specifications and with any bells and whistles of your choosing from several manufacturers. When a part broke or wore out, those that weren't kept on warehouse shelves could be ordered and installed in a matter of hours or days. Even in 1958, steam locomotives required shops employing scores of blacksmiths and other craftsmen whose very titles conjured up images of the era of the horse and buggy.

The new president of the Norfolk & Western Railway, Stuart T. Saunders, a man who had come from the mountains of West Virginia—the quintessential coal-mining state—was anything but a sentimentalist when it came to steam locomotives. In an age when piston-driven airliners were being replaced with jets, there was no place for the huffing, puffing teakettles that roamed the N&W rails like so many dinosaurs. According to noted N&W historian and Salem, Virginia resident Kenneth Miller, "His [Saunders's] first actions were to remove all images of a steam engine from everything having anything to do with the N&W."[65] Until the railroad's order for new diesel-electrics could be fulfilled, it would lease them from other railroads that could spare motive power. This included the RF&P and Atlantic Coast Line, whose Florida-bound passenger service soared in the winter but ebbed during the summer months.

Saunders, a hard-nosed businessman, had no illusions either about the role of passenger trains on his railroad: they lost money—especially branch line locals—and thus, in his opinion, they had to go.

With those thoughts in mind, Gene Luck placed a call to his counterpart in Roanoke. While waiting for him to answer, Luck's thoughts turned to the hundreds of images that the N&W had produced that immortalized the role of the steam locomotive, including the series of classic pictures by well-known industrial photographer O. Winston Link.

Luck was uncertain whether the N&W would even consider a venture whose purpose was to draw crowds to ride its trains.

"Yes?" the voice on the other end of the phone evidently answered. If Miller & Rhoads was willing to underwrite the cost of operating them, he could see no reason why N&W senior management would object. As long as they didn't interfere with the railroad's coal and freight business and didn't cost anything, why should they?

Luck conveyed the good news to the marketing managers at Miller & Rhoads but was surprised when they made an additional request: would he serve as a liaison, a technical advisor, to implement the Roanoke Santa Train on the Norfolk & Western? He'd see what he could do, but they had to understand that his first responsibility was to generate sales of tickets on the RF&P's passenger trains. RF&P, after all, was paying his salary. And while his initial arrangement had been made with W. Thomas Rice Jr., who had just been elevated to the presidency of the Atlantic Coast Line Railroad, he owed no less diligence to the RF&P's new chief executive, Wirt P. Marks Jr. Yes, he would assist them in any way possible, if the RF&P agreed.

There was something else adding to the complexity of the Santa Train operations in 1958, other than the planning for another Santa Special from Ashland for Cox Incorporated and the Miller & Rhoads trains. J.C.Penney, a national retailer with stores in Virginia, was interested in sponsoring Santa Trains to cater to the customers who shopped at its downtown Alexandria store. Additionally, the Retail Merchants of Fredericksburg had notified Gene Luck that they would dearly love for Santa Claus to arrive in their city on a special RF&P train.

Logistically, both trains from Alexandria and Fredericksburg, following the model he had established with the Miller & Rhoads trains, could pick up Santa at some point en route and reverse directions at Quantico. There, the RF&P train dispatcher could use signals to line the route. With a push of the buttons on his desk, he could direct the trains into a siding. There, technicians would be able to quickly perform the mechanical work necessary to reposition the locomotives on the opposite end of the train, in order to make the return trip to Alexandria or Fredericksburg. The RF&P might have been a comparatively small railroad in terms of length, but it was on the cutting edge of technology. It was the first U.S. railroad to have the ability to control movement over its entire main line using the controls contained in a single office at a central location. It was light-years ahead of the competition.[66]

The only challenge was being able to schedule those same twenty passenger cars for use up and down the railroad on dates that would be compatible. As it was, the 1958 Cox Santa Train was scheduled for Saturday afternoon, December 6, whereas the previous Santa Special had departed Ashland at 7:30 p.m. on a Friday. Clearly, for families with small children, when the train finally arrived back into town, it was way past some people's bed times. The request was understandable.

There were also home games scheduled for the Washington Redskins National Football League franchise to consider. The Skins were reputed to be so bad that Luck's only limit for the number of tickets the team would front him was the number of seats on his trains that he could sell. Washington had become a perennial occupant of the league's basement. It appeared they only existed to serve as an opponent for another team to play. Still, Richmonders flocked to Broad Street Station on Sunday mornings to board those special trains, and as long as they did, the RF&P would gladly accept their money—no matter who won the game. As Bill Deekens, author Donna Strother Deekens's husband, was quick to add, "One of my neighbors in Petersburg rode the Redskins train for every game in the 1960s and truly enjoyed himself, whether they won or lost."[67] And in spite of the fact that the Redskins usually lost, the mood of those coming back to Richmond on the return trip was festive. Most were well behaved. And sometimes, the Skins actually won. (Coincidentally, in 2013, the Washington Redskins established their summer training facility on land that was once part of the Broad Street Station complex, in Richmond.)

All of those scheduling conflicts could be resolved, however. Right now, Luck had to make a trip to Roanoke to meet with Norfolk & Western management and take a look at the railroad to determine how best to launch Miller & Rhoads' newest Santa Train. Also, they would have to determine where it was to run and what would be required as far as locomotives and coaches.

There was no doubt in anyone's mind that where trains were concerned, Roanoke was a slam-dunk. The only people who didn't draw a paycheck from the Norfolk & Western Railway were the people who bagged the groceries, pumped the gas and sold the clothes worn by those who did.

For most young men about to graduate from high school in the area, the choice was not necessarily what college they planned to attend so much as in what department of the N&W they wished to work: operations, signals, mechanical or maintenance of way. Those who ranked in the upper percentiles of their classes would most likely be able to land a job among the clerical ranks. Those who truly excelled would be candidates for the railroad's management-training program. Those going on to college would find local institutions of higher learning offering a curriculum that prepared them for engineering and finance.

In 1958, the doors of opportunity were opening for young women as well. Whereas in the not-so-distant past, secretarial positions were awarded to men, it was becoming more common for the N&W Roanoke ranks to have female graduates with high school or college diplomas—possibly influenced by women participating in the workforce during the war. It would be decades however, before their faces would appear in locomotive cabs or along the right of way.

Luck passed the impressive Miller & Rhoads downtown Roanoke store at the corner of Campbell and Henry Streets on his way to the N&W offices: solid, conservative—very Virginian in appearance. It was very much like the RF&P, he thought, a good match and good people with whom to do business.

There was an odd smell in the air—coal smoke. Since the RF&P had done away with the last of its own steam locomotives in 1953, two years before Luck came to work for them, it was an unusual scent and scene, even though the N&W did operate steam locomotives into Broad Street Station in Richmond. But, looking down from the hills of Roanoke onto the N&W's extensive tracks and shops, Luck was reminded of his own childhood in Alabama, where his dad had worked as a railroad clerk.[68]

When it comes to trains, men are simply boys with a bit more sophisticated degree of curiosity. Give them an unobstructed view of a railroad yard or a passenger station, and they'll stand there and watch until they're convinced that there's nothing more to see.

"There won't be many more of them still breath'n steam here before long," a stranger intoned as Luck stood looking at the movement below. "Understand they're going to lease diesels from the Atlantic Coast Line and the RF&P this summer to get rid of the last of the steam engines on our passengers trains."

"You work for the N&W?" Luck asked the man.

"No, I'm a banker, taking my lunch break. My dad did, and his dad before him. Here in Roanoke, and up into the mountains where they mine coal, those steam engines are our steam engines. It's gonna seem sorta strange without 'em," the man said, his voice trailing off, as if he were talking about an infirm older member of the family. Luck wanted to tell the man that he worked for the RF&P but thought better of it and simply wished him a good day before walking toward the railroad's offices to keep his appointment.

Gene Luck's meeting with the N&W passenger and operating personnel went smoothly. Mr. J.V. Fagan, N&W's passenger traffic manager, explained that based on what they'd discussed during their prior phone conversations, a stretch of track between Roanoke and Elliston had been identified as the place best suited for their needs. The train would make a stop at Salem, just outside town, where Santa and the Snow Queen would board. They would continue on to Elliston, where they would reverse direction and return to Roanoke.

There would be ample equipment for the train since a sizeable number of applications for discontinuance of passenger service had been granted. And unless something drastic occurred, the N&W would be using diesel locomotives—not steam.

Luck had to wonder what would have happened if he'd applied for a job in passenger service sales at the N&W, rather than with the RF&P. He probably questioned what N&W president Stuart Saunders's reaction would have been compared to what RF&P president Tom Rice's was. If he had gone to N&W, would he even have a job with a railroad, or would he still be hawking grocery bags out of that 1937 Buick? Rice came from an engineering background on a railroad that was committed to passenger service. Saunders had come up through the ranks of the law department on a railroad that had wonderful passenger trains but didn't serve the same large East Coast cities or the subtropical beach resorts of Florida's east and west coasts. One saw passenger service as a complement to his railroad's freight business. The other viewed it as an impediment to his company's bottom line.

Either way, Luck would let the management of Miller & Rhoads know that it was feasible to operate the Santa Train to promote its Roanoke location. Other aspects of the joint venture were up to them.

CHAPTER 11

MAMA SAYS

Anyone who has ever watched his or her spouse flustered and in a total dither over what to wear to an event whose invitation simply reads, "come as you are," can surely empathize with the parents of the young children of Roanoke, Virginia, in the weeks and days leading up to the city's very first Miller & Rhoads Santa Train. December 6, 1958, was going to be quite a day, indeed. There had been a run on tickets ever since the ads began appearing in the *Roanoke Times*, announcing that a special Norfolk & Western passenger train would be departing the downtown station on an excursion to pick up jolly ol' Saint Nick and his Snow Queen and deliver them to the star city. Tickets were available only at Miller & Rhoads, the ad noted—not at the N&W station. And only a limited number were available.

Recalled Mrs. Claudine Miller, the wife of an N&W conductor, "As soon as I saw the ad in the paper, I went right down there and got enough tickets for my son, Kenneth, and his cousin, Ginger, who was four years older than he was. They've always been really close. We got there early, too."[69]

To be sure, the phone lines were burning up with anxious moms, questioning their little girls' best friends' mothers. "I mean, it's a train trip, so you know they should be well dressed, but how well dressed?" In the 1950s (just as was the custom in the early days of commercial air travel), men wore coats and ties. Women adorned their heads with hats. It was almost as if the entire family were taking the day coach to Sunday school and morning worship services.

Young train enthusiast Kenneth Miller visits with Santa in the Miller & Rhoads downtown Roanoke, Virginia store, 1959. *Kenneth Miller Private Collection.*

"I can't remember," Julia Steward Milton, of Christiansburg, Virginia, wrote in a letter. "Knowing my mother, I am sure we were dressed in sweet little Christmas dresses with crinoline slips and shiny little shoes (maybe even hats and white gloves!). Our mother was such a pretty woman. No matter how cute we looked that day, I doubt we could have competed with her."[70]

Convincing excited little girls to go dress shopping with their mothers was relatively easy. Trying to get boys like little Kenneth Miller to go inside the downtown Roanoke Miller & Rhoads store to find something suitable to wear on the train was a virtual tug of war. One of his fondest memories was the Miller & Rhoads train window. Some sixty years later, his mother, Claudine, like the mothers of every young boy who came within eyesight of that corner train window, had to contend with her son's fascination for trains and his insistence on remaining outside to watch every engine and every car.

Store manager at that time, George Bryson, recalls that the corner window of the Roanoke store was every bit as fine as the one at their flagship store's train window at Fifth and Grace Streets in Richmond. This fantasyland—the product of some master window dresser's imagination—was a diorama depicting the commonwealth of Virginia as an intricate labyrinth of bridges, tunnels, towers and waterways. It was accented by twirling beacons and flashing crossing gates. O scale Lionel trains, as well as more-detailed, half-sized HO gauge trains, sped from one end of state to the other.[71]

Moms like Claudine Miller had to beg their sons or daughters to come inside the store with them so that they could find suitable coats for them to wear aboard the Santa Train.

"Just a couple minutes more, Mom, please?" was the most often-spoken phrase heard outside the Miller & Rhoads store.

If he was like most young boys in the N&W's headquarters city, Kenneth had a special place in his heart for the engines most associated with his dad's employer—the famous J-class, bullet-nosed, streamlined passenger locomotives built in the railroad's massive Roanoke shops, just a couple blocks away from where they were standing.[72] You have to wonder just how many Lionel J-class steam locomotives still occupy playrooms (and attics) in the Greater Roanoke area half a century later. Most likely, there's one in every home.

Lots of boys, their noses pressed up against the cold glass of the huge display window, had already made up their minds to ask Santa to make sure he brought them one when they saw him on the Santa Train. And Santa most likely did just that. Maybe the Santa Train would even be pulled by a J.

December 6 dawned. It took the sun a bit longer to illuminate the valley below because it had to climb the tall mountains that surrounded the town to get a peak at the carpet of homes that spread from one side to the other. Lights were already on. The aroma of fresh-brewed coffee, frying bacon and eggs drifted from one house to the next. Thick biscuits had already popped from the ovens in most homes in the area.

Roanoke was not the type of town that waited for the sun to rise. It was one in which the alarm clock sounded in total darkness, where feet hit the floor as one hand searched for the light switch and another fumbled on the nightstand for a lighter and a pack of cigarettes. At this time of the morning—or in the middle of the night, depending on your perspective—men showered, shaved and donned freshly washed pairs of bib overalls. Before they could sit down to breakfast, their black metal lunch boxes had been packed with an assortment of sandwiches, cakes and fruit. On the kitchen counter near the back door, standing like a sentry keeping guard, was a large Thermos, filled to the top with enough coffee to make it through lunch and the ability to keep it warm until "quitin' time."

This Saturday morning was special. A town whose entire economy was based on the ability of a flanged wheel to turn on a steel rail was to play host to its families and those of its neighbors. It was an opportunity for the railroad to pull back the curtains for a behind-the-scenes peek at what goes on backstage. The Miller & Rhoads Santa Train—two diesel locomotives and twenty-four coach cars—was already standing at the Roanoke station. Like a scene from a classic old movie, steam escaped from valves beneath the cars and from the connections between them. Headlights and brakes had been tested to make certain they worked properly.

This would be no ordinary passenger train. Not only would it be carrying the wives and children of hundreds of railroad employees—many making their first ever journey by train—but also along the way, it was understood that the jolly ol' elf himself would climb aboard to be transported in grand fashion into town. Along the route, the faithful would be granted an audience with the man who made dreams come true.

Ginger Hibbetts Sweet paced the floor anxiously, stopping each time she passed the front door of her home to see if the car carrying her Aunt Claudine and cousin Ken had somehow managed to quietly pull up to the curb of her house undetected.

"I remember it so well," she said. "I was about four years older than Ken, and we were very close. When they asked me to go with them on the Santa

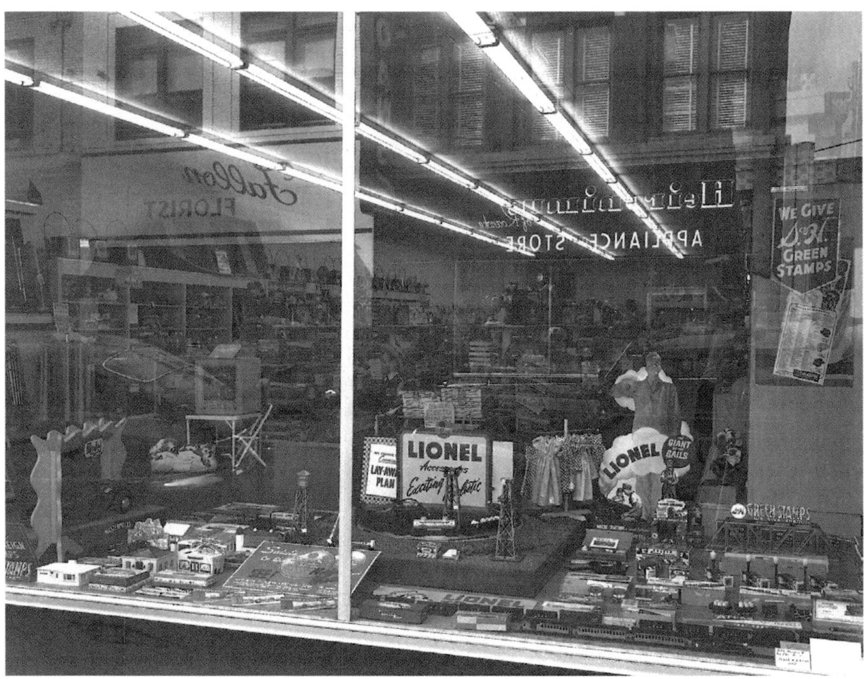

Jennings-Shepherd sporting goods store in Roanoke, Virginia, devoted its storefront window to a holiday Lionel train display, November 1952. *Kenneth Miller Private Collection.*

Train, it was so very special to me. We didn't have a lot of money to spend growing up, so I was thrilled to be a part of this!"

Ginger went on to recall, "My mother helped me coordinate everything that included my best dress, tights, black patent leather shoes, mittens and a wool coat. The coat was a must because it was so cold!"

As her aunt's car pulled up in front of Ginger's home, she remembered her mother's admonishment: "Don't tear your tights!"[73]

The N&W station sat across from the Hotel Roanoke. There was no similarity of design, however. The exposed timbers of the grand hotel reminded visitors of a Swiss ski chalet they might find tucked into the side of the snow-topped Alps. The modern glass, steel and concrete depot, however, conveyed a sense of no-nonsense twentieth-century travel. It was intended to complement the railroad's streamlined locomotives. Ever since the coming of the diesels, the N&W had fought a battle—not only for itself but also on behalf of its customers—attempting to convince a world that tended to view coal as a throwback to a bygone era that it was, in fact, a timeless resource that could adapt to any future.

For young Ginger, the Miller & Rhoads Santa Train was her first-ever train ride. "It was a real treat in itself!" she added.[74]

It had been a long time since so many people had crowded the station. Passenger traffic on the N&W had dropped 50 percent between 1949 and 1955, according to the book on the railroad's passenger service that would be written years later by none other than Kenneth Miller.[75] This was the same young man who accompanied his cousin down the steps to the platform, where the seemingly endless ribbon of polished Tuscan red passenger cars was assembled. Ginger and Ken took a seat together, just as the train began to move.

"There were activities going on the entire time that kept us busy. There was Christmas music and clowns. We were given coloring books and candy canes," Mrs. Sweet noted excitedly.

Not too terribly far outside town, at the quaint little station of Salem, the train came to a halt. There on the platform stood Santa Claus and the Snow Queen. The sight caused pause not only for the passengers but also for the crew members of one of the railroad's local freight trains, who stopped their labor for a moment while the white-bearded gent from up north and his beautiful traveling companion posed beside the rear vestibule of the Santa Train for a newspaper photographer before climbing aboard. The looks on the railroad men's faces screamed a deep degree of pride, although not a word was spoken. This was their train, their railroad and their town.

The nearly two thousand people aboard looked toward the rear of the train as though they had but one set of eyes—all were on the doors that they anticipated would burst open to reveal the storied man in red they'd all come to see. "He came through the train, greeting adults as well as children," Ginger Sweet remembered.[76]

"I remember the Snow Queen more so than Santa," admitted Julia Stewart Milton. "Perhaps it was because at that time, I was fascinated with 'bride' dolls, and she was dressed in white and so beautiful."[77]

Rounding the long curve coming into Elliston, the Miller & Rhoads Santa Train slowed and finally eased to a stop. Quickly, out of sight of the revelers aboard, a group of railroad workers descended on the point at which the two locomotives were coupled to the rest of the train. Like a bunch of Santa's elves, they began hammering on the pipes and hoses through which steam and compressed air traveled to the train to operate its brakes and provide heat. The engines pulled away from the train, leaving it momentarily, as it was switched to the adjacent track and operated to the other end of the train. Then, it was switched back to the track on which the Santa Train

Santa and the Snow Queen pose before boarding the N&W/Miller & Rhoads Santa Train at Salem, Virginia, in December 1959. *Kenneth Miller Private Collection.*

stood. There, after being coupled to it, the same army of men in overalls began tapping on the pipes and hoses necessary to reconnect the air and steam supply to the train. Once OKed, and after everyone was safely in the clear, the Miller & Rhoads Santa Train began rolling slowly back down the mountain toward Roanoke.

"I thought we had gone to Radford," Mrs. Milton said, "but apparently we went only as far as Elliston. When you're younger, everything seems bigger and longer. Whatever it might actually have been, it certainly seemed magical to us."

Julia Stewart Milton's most precious memory was "my sister and I having such wonderful parents who made this special adventure possible for us!"[78]

Our special memories of the Miller & Rhoads Roanoke Santa Train were made for us on April 20, 2013, when we traveled to Salem, Virginia—the same town where Saint Nick and the beautiful Snow Queen had boarded fifty-five years earlier. There, we visited with Mrs. Claudine Miller, her son, Ken, and his wife, Beth. As Mrs. Miller sat there in a chair by a huge picture window that allowed her a vista of the valley she'd called home for so many years, the words came a bit slowly but the memories were as crystal clear as if they'd happened just that morning. The fact that she tired easily could almost have been attributed to having risen early that morning to take her curious little son, Ken, and her niece, Ginger, for a ride on the Santa Train. Truly, she remembered in great detail the events of the two years—1958 and

1959—when she made it a point to rise early to secure those tickets. With this gift, her family not only experienced the majesty of the Virginia mountains and the Shenandoah Valley from the window of a rumbling coach car but was also touched by Santa's magic as the special train made its way from Roanoke to the "North Pole" and back.

There were local celebrities aboard as well, Mrs. Miller said, with a sly smile that belied a coming punch line. "The first year, there were personalities from the local television station aboard. There was 'Cactus Joe' and 'Miss Kathy' from *Romper Room*. And there was this little fella who was dressed as an elf. His job was to follow Santa through the train to hand out coloring books and paper engineers' hats to the children. [He] said he was Santa Claus's cousin—Santi Flush [Sani Flush was the brand name of a popular bathroom cleanser of the time]. I recall that he looked as if he was having the best time of anyone on the train!" she laughed.[79]

Thank heavens for a late Christmas present I purchased for myself, just before we traveled to Salem—a small, compact video recorder that I set up on a tripod to document Claudine Miller's remarks. Our written words simply cannot do justice to those she spoke that day. As Ken and his wife, Beth, and the coauthors, Donna Strother Deekens and Doug Riddell, packed up our belongings and headed for the door to dine at a favorite local eatery, we gave Mrs. Miller a big hug. As she made her way down the hallway toward her bedroom for her afternoon nap, she stopped, turned, looked at us, smiled and said, "Don't forget his name now, Santi Flush!" The gleam in her eye said it all.

Not long after that, we received a message from Ken Miller. His mother had become ill and was hospitalized. Days later, another message showed up on my computer, announcing the passing of Mrs. Claudine Miller. It was as if she'd waited all of those years to share her story. We're thankful for her patience. The wait was well worth it.

In a letter from N&W's manager of passenger traffic, dated December 9, 1958, Gene Luck found encouragement in J.V. Fagan's words, "You will probably be interested to know that the Santa Claus Promotional Trains operated from Roanoke, Va. to Elliston, VA, and return on Saturday, December 6th, sponsored by Miller & Rhoads, were considered a complete success. Four thousand and nineteen tickets were sold and the first train by actual count handled 1,890 passengers and the second train 1,866.

"I want you to know that we greatly appreciate having received the idea from you and the benefit of your expertise in operating these trains. We

The Miller & Rhoads lapel button, with bright red ribbon, was a Christmas greeting identifying employees in all stores, circa 1960s. *Lewis Parks Private Collection.*

hope to operate similar trains in the future. I hope the trains which you operated out of Richmond this year were a complete success."[80]

Those words sounded so promising that no one could have anticipated that the Roanoke Miller & Rhoads Santa Trains would operate for only one more year.

"When the [N&W] railroad presented the proposed cost of operating the Santa Trains to us for 1960, the expense was outrageous. They said that the increased cost was due to switching from steam engines to diesels," a saddened and perplexed George Bryson said in an interview at his home in 2013. "They just didn't want to be bothered with us."[81]

Sadly, the only J-class steam locomotives operating in Roanoke in December 1960 were those circling the base of a thousand little boys' Christmas trees and the one in the corner window of the Miller & Rhoads store. In 1959, the Santa Train halted for the final time at the Roanoke,

Virginia station. After Santa, the Snow Queen, the clowns, the elves and the thousands of parents and children had all gone home to enjoy the holiday season, the only trains that would stop to pick up Santa and the Snow Queen at Salem were those in the snow-globe memories of Julia Stewart Milton, Ginger Hibbetts Sweet, Ken Miller and Claudine Miller—and perhaps even Santa's mischievous little elf, Santi Flush.

CHAPTER 12

STALLING

To the east of Roanoke stood the city of Lynchburg. Astride the same James River that snaked downward through the hills and valleys of the lush green Virginia Piedmont to the state capital of Richmond, it had no large railroad shops. It was, however, still a railroad town. Loaded trains bound for the port of Hampton Roads and unending consists of empty hopper cars headed for another bellyful of Virginia and West Virginia coal mingled at different levels on three different lines that visited the city. The Southern Railway, which connected Washington, D.C., with Atlanta, New Orleans and the great majority of the South, headed north from its downtown station, vaulting high above the banks of the James. Far below, the Chesapeake & Ohio Railway's steel thruway clung to its banks, sometimes regretfully. When the waterway would swell after a heavy or prolonged period of rain, the James often reached out to reclaim what had rightfully been its own. The adjacent canal, constructed on its north bank, was intended to connect eastern ports with the Ohio River and had resulted from a survey conducted by a young George Washington. A successor to the canal company, the railroad was laid on the canal's towpath as far as Richmond. The C&O was later extended by industrialist Collis P. Huntington to the deep-water port of Newport News and later to the Midwest.

The N&W passenger route through Lynchburg ran side by side with the C&O, along the river shore into Union Station, before it ascended from the floor of the valley in an intense storm of smoke and sand, attempting to conquer the hills to its west. By 1959, a fleet of whining red diesel locomotives

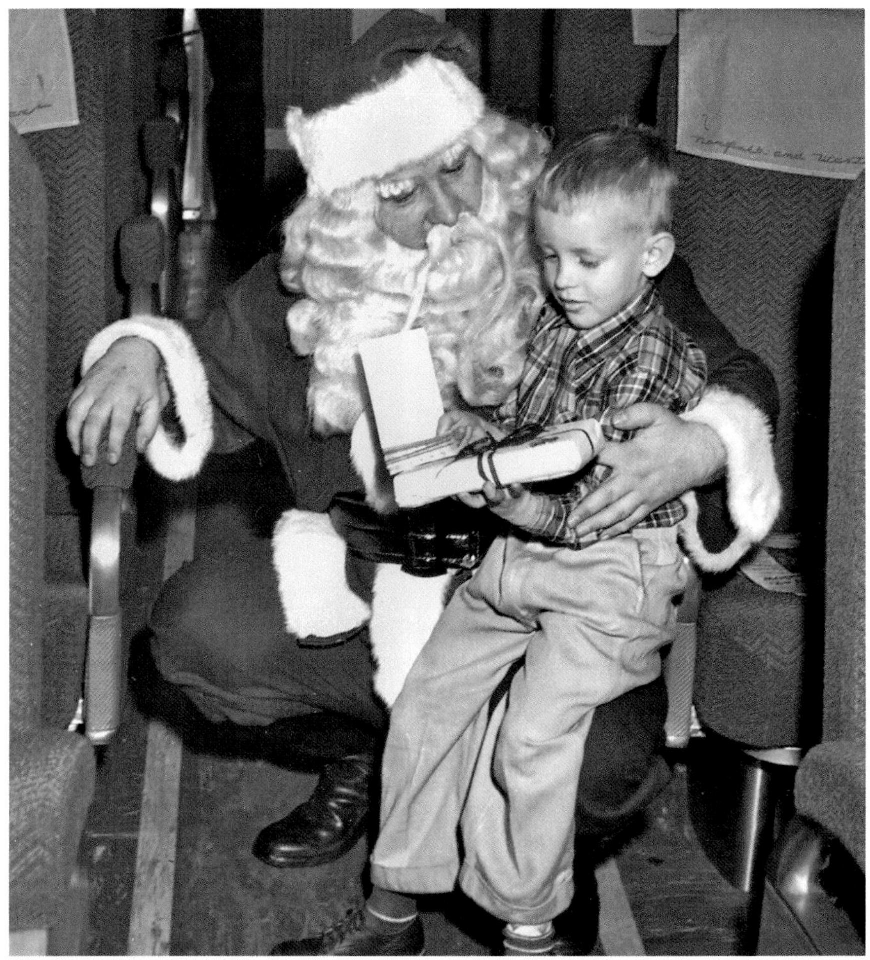

Santa stops to greet a young boy aboard a Norfolk & Western train, circa 1950s. *Courtesy Norfolk Southern Corp.*

continued the battle of the grades that had been waged for decades by powerful steam engines making their way to Roanoke. There, they would pause for a momentary respite before charging up the peaks west of town en route to the communities in the coals fields of West Virginia, Cincinnati and onward to the ports of the Great Lakes.

The number of different railroads and picturesque elevations made for interesting model railroad possibilities, and to that end, little boys and their fathers visited local merchants, such as Baldwin's department store. There,

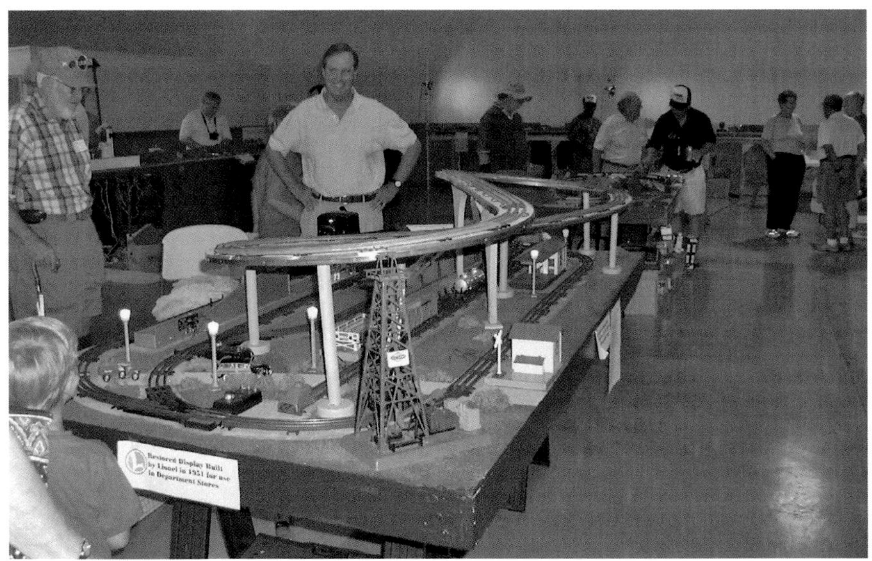

Bernard Baldwin hosts a display of a restored 1950s Lionel exhibit at Lynchburg's "Rail Day," August 11, 2007. *Courtesy Blue Ridge Chapter, National Railway Historical Society.*

they would check out the latest engines, cars and layouts from Lionel to get ideas for what to incorporate in their setup beneath the Christmas tree.

Miller & Rhoads had a downtown Lynchburg store there as well, and in 1959, buoyed by the success of the Santa Trains that had been operated by the N&W on its behalf the previous year, the store eyed a similar promotion. John Burnett of the Lynchburg store and Gary Barnum of the Roanoke store enthusiastically coordinated the details of the proposed trains with the N&W.[82]

It was decided that the Roanoke train would operate two round trips to Elliston on Saturday, December 5, as it had done the year before—one at 10:00 a.m. and one at 1:00 p.m.—stopping in nearby Salem to board Santa and his Snow Queen. Using the same equipment and following the same departure schedule the following week, on December 12, the twenty-four-car special would depart Lynchburg's Union Station at the foot of Ninth Street. From there, it would head west to Halsey Siding, where a stop would be made to pick up Mr. Claus and the radiant Snow Queen for a trip that would mean turning back at Forest.

Saturday, December 12, arrived and, with it, the same N&W engines and coaches that had performed flawlessly the preceding week at Roanoke. This year there was an even broader array of local television celebrities on board.

"Uncle Looney," "Barker Bill," "Bozo the Clown" and "Cactus Joe" hobknobbed with the youngsters who marveled at them on TV. Along with thirteen attractive young ladies dressed as elves, or "Santa's Helpers," they began distributing coloring books and handing out candy canes.

According to an account in the employees' *N&W Railway* magazine, in the following months, representatives from the railroad's passenger services and transportation departments became kids again, helping out by taking up tickets and assisting Santa's Helpers.

What had not been taken into account was the extreme grade used by passenger trains that accessed Union Station in Lynchburg, which curved from the riverfront platform and through a valley to crest a hill. Most of the railroad's freight trains, which did not have reason to use the station, did not have to face the steep rise that the Santa Train would find itself battling with two locomotives and twenty-four coaches.

To compound the problem, Santa and the Snow Queen would be waiting at Halsey Siding, just past the Langhorne Road trestle. Whereas most trains would have been able to get a good run at the hill, the Santa Train would be stopping to enable its special guests to board on the side of a very steep grade.

Lee Hawkins, in his early teens, was the son of an N&W railroader and, as he recalls, "rode along for the fun of it." Sitting in the station, Hawkins noted just how long the train extended. "The rear car was near, if not blocking, the C&O railroad crossing."[83] While this would in no way have endangered anyone, it did mean that any C&O trains wishing to use that track would have to wait until the Santa Train, occupying the N&W tracks, had moved on before they could proceed.

The Miller & Rhoads special departed promptly at 10:00 a.m. with no signs of a problem until it neared Halsey Siding. There, in addition to making a stop, the engineer had been told to slow the train to a crawl, in order for the children on board to get a good view of Saint Nick as he and the Snow Queen came into sight.

"Well, almost no problem," chuckled Lee Hawkins, when one of us spoke to him by phone. "I think the train had hardly moved when someone pulled the emergency cord, and this rather rotund lady, walking down the aisle, took a huge tumble. She must have rolled halfway through the car before she was able to stop." After that, the train resumed its assault on the hilly terrain leaving Lynchburg's upper James River basin.

Only a locomotive engineer can appreciate what happened next, as explained in a conversation with Hawkins: "After Santa and his Snow Queen boarded, we sat for about thirty minutes or so because the engines had a problem pulling out of Halsey, I guess because of the grade." N&W had extra personnel riding that train to ensure that nothing went wrong. According to Hawkins, "My dad said that if we hadn't had a couple of electricians and mechanics on board, we'd still be sitting on the side of that hill."[84]

Like *The Little Engine That Could*, the engineer of the Miller & Rhoads Santa Train was able to get it to move, then creep and finally gain enough speed to top the hill and pull into Forest. The very relieved N&W staff was able to disconnect the locomotives and move them from the front of the train to its rear for the return trip to Lynchburg.

Next time, however, there were three red N&W locomotives leading the train, and instead of stopping at Halsey, Santa and the Snow Queen boarded the Lynchburg Miller & Rhoads Santa Train at Forest. As a result, everything went off without a hitch.

John F. Wranek, general manager of the Lynchburg Miller & Rhoads store, expressed his appreciation for the N&W's performance in a letter to the railroad's passenger traffic department. In part, he said, "I want to commend your Norfolk & Western representative[s] for their grand cooperation. They worked with us in every way and deserved a large share of the credit for the success of the train.

"Your 'giveaways' [N&W and Association of American Railroad booklets] were most effective, and I hope you and your associates feel that this was a very worth-while public relations event. We would like to plan for a bigger and better Santa train in 1960, and we will keep in touch with you."[85]

There was no Miller & Rhoads Lynchburg or Roanoke Santa Train in 1960, however. As previously mentioned, George Bryson, the Roanoke store's manager, was stunned when he was told that there would be a substantial increase in the cost of the trains' operation by N&W "because of the switch from steam to diesel."[86] Since Miller & Rhoads' Santa Trains were never operated with steam locomotives (so far as anyone knows), the higher costs must have resulted from the railroad's internal pricing structure. Our expertise does not extend into the intricacies of high finance.

Looking back on the faces of the young riders of the short-lived N&W Miller & Rhoads Santa Trains, we can only echo the sentiments of Mrs. Claudine Miller, who said, "It was always such a great time for the adults and children, as well. I can't understand why they would want to stop running them."[87]

To dear Mrs. Miller, we say, neither can we.

CHAPTER 13

1960 ENDINGS AND BEGINNINGS

The year 1960 was a watershed Christmas season for Santa Claus Trains. They had begun to take root and grow in Richmond, probably because the Miller & Rhoads flagship store was there and top management was immediately available to address any concerns, in addition to the fact that the executive offices of the Richmond, Fredericksburg & Potomac Railroad were just a scant twenty blocks away at Broad Street Station. But more than likely, it was probably in large part because of the relationship that had been forged between Gene Luck and the marketing and promotion leadership at the store. Richmond has always been that type of town—a comparatively large city with an amiable business community, whose associations do not end at quitting time.

In the competitive environment of sales, it is quite an honor to be cited as the best salesman in your store or district. You can imagine the surprise and delight that abounded on the RF&P when Gordon Mallonee, vice-president of promotions for Miller & Rhoads, summoned Luck to the store's executive offices, where Mallonee presented Luck with a trophy for the "Best Sales Promotion for the Week." It was noted that Gene Luck was not only the first nonemployee ever to be accorded such an honor but also that the vote by the store's executives was unanimous.[88]

In an early 1959 RF&P *Rail-O-Gram*, the railroad went on to praise Luck because he had traveled to Roanoke to work with officials of the Norfolk & Western Railway and Miller & Rhoads on its sister project.

All of the good luck in the world could not change the fortunes of Cox Incorporated, however. As much as its management would have loved to continue the Santa Special tradition it had pioneered and as proud as Ashland was of its endeavor, it simply could not afford to do so in 1959. Sadly, the doors of the Cox store closed in 1960.

Nor could all of the publicly aired smiles and praise hide the divide that had privately developed between the N&W and Miller & Rhoads over operating-cost increases. In the long run, no compromise to continue the Santa Trains in Roanoke or Lynchburg could be reached for 1960, although, as Miller & Rhoads noted, all four 1959 trains had been sellouts. As retired Miller & Rhoads executive George Bryson reiterated sadly when we spoke with him recently at his Richmond home, "At the price the railroad was asking, the stores' sales volumes simply couldn't justify the expense."[89]

At the northern terminus of the RF&P though, the J.C. Penney store in Alexandria was in a stronger position. It represented that large national chain in the booming and affluent Northern Virginia suburbs in 1960. While the fortunes of Richmond fluctuated with the sales of cigarettes and the volatility of the financial markets, the communities that lived literally in the shadow of the capitol dome were insulated from most upheavals, save for the change of presidential administrations every four years. Even then, while some of the heads of various departments might have changed, the day-to-day operations of government soldiered on. The Northern Virginia suburbs of Alexandria, Arlington and Fairfax County were home to the people who wrote the tax codes, kept track of budgets, issued checks and generally greased the wheels of democracy. The presence of the military in and around the Pentagon also accounted for a very large, but very transient, chunk of the population.

Having seen the positive results of the Miller & Rhoads Santa Train, the management of the downtown Alexandria J.C. Penney store was receptive to the invitation from RF&P's Gene Luck to have its own Santa Train in 1958. In keeping with the model he had perfected, the store would have the benefit of the foot traffic that the train's ticket sales would generate.

Operationally, while the railroad's primary base, at which its passenger equipment and locomotives were kept and serviced, was one hundred miles to the south in Richmond, the equipment could be readied and brought to Alexandria in about two hours. There, it would be parked on one of two main line tracks in front of the small Union Station and prepared to board and depart southbound for Quantico thirty minutes later. Santa would be waiting at the small community of Newington, a Spartan station on the

Nº 372 Penney's

SANTA CLAUS TRAIN

on the R.F.&P. Railroad

LEAVES ALEXANDRIA, VA. – 2:00 P. M.

SATURDAY, NOVEMBER 28, 1970.

$1.50 each – No Refunds or Exchanges

One needed to purchase a ticket at J.C. Penney for the Santa Train that left Union Station in Alexandria, Virginia, 1970. *Chuck McIntyre Private Collection.*

fringes of the sprawling military reservation of Fort Belvoir. From there it would continue to a siding just north of the town made famous as the home of the United States Marines and the training facility for the Federal Bureau of Investigation.

In an area noted for naming its estuaries after the Native American tribes that once hunted in its woodlands and fished from its sparkling clean streams, a switching location called Possum Point does tend to get one's attention. Opposite Quantico Creek from a civilian business district populated with barbershops advertising military haircuts and taverns, the railroad had a small yard made up of three or four tracks. There, it delivered trains comprised entirely of coal that powered the massive Possum Point electric generating plant. As was done with the Santa Trains at Doswell, the three J.C. Penney schedules would reverse direction by removing the diesel locomotives from the south end of the cars and reattaching them to the north end for the trip back to Alexandria.

At day's end, the locomotives and empty coach cars would make their return to Richmond. Those same twenty cars that Gene Luck apparently snatched from the jaws of a scrap yard cutting torch would again host thousands of young children, scores of elves, clowns and Santa on a cold Saturday in December. Luck was almost becoming a victim of his own success—there were only so many dates on which to schedule Santa Trains. Fortunately, the Redskins played on Sundays and the Senators and Orioles' baseball season did not extend into the winter months.

Walter Loftin was a ticket agent at the Alexandria station during some of the years that the J.C. Penney Santa Train operated. Among his other duties—after the ads appeared in the paper announcing the dates and times when the trains would operate—it was necessary for him to remind some parents that tickets were available only at the downtown Alexandria J.C. Penney store—not at the quaint brick station's ticket window. In several telephone interviews with coauthor Doug Riddell, he recalled the thrill of seeing the platform and station crowded with parents and children.[90]

One family that rode the train annually for many years was a couple and their two daughters, who made their way from a home on Glebe Road near Washington National Airport to the station after having secured their tickets early at Penney's.

"Did I ride the Santa Train?" Hanover County schoolteacher Jacqueline Stewart laughed. "You bet. Our Sundays were spent sitting on the grassy hill at the Alexandria station next to the tracks with Mom and Dad, watching the trains come and go for hours and hours. We rode the Santa Train every year for as long as I can remember."

While she couldn't think of any memories that stood out—"They were all special, although I can't cite specifics"—she responded that "I wish my mother were here. She would remember every detail."[91] That, in and of itself, is special.

Mrs. Stewart is dear to the heart of one of her students, Ryan Riddell, author Doug Riddell's son. She took a special interest in him at Rural Point Elementary School, possibly because his young world revolved completely around trains. Over the years, the Riddells remained in touch with Mrs. Stewart, and to no one's surprise—especially not Jackie Stewart's—after high school graduation, at age eighteen, Ryan Riddell became an Amtrak conductor and, today, is an Amtrak engineer.

Like the Richmond trains, the J.C. Penney Alexandria Santa Trains grew steadily in popularity. During the 1960s, the demand for tickets resulted in the RF&P expanding its special trains' schedules to accommodate Santa Trains as early as late November in order to provide opportunities in which to schedule them. An RF&P *Rail-O-Gram* for 1967 noted that on November 25, there were three trains operating between Alexandria and Possum Point carrying 3,800 passengers. Other years saw two and three trains run on two consecutive weekends.[92]

Alexandria resident Dale Latham, a youngster at the time, not only rode some of the Santa Trains but also lived near the RF&P tracks and grew up watching them from his back porch: "We originally lived near the station but later moved to the west end of Alexandria, near Cameron Run." Cameron Run is a pleasant creek that sometimes spills out of its banks, flooded by rain from the surrounding hills that collects in the narrow ravine through which it flows. It is also the point at which the RF&P leaves Alexandria and begins its assault on the very steep curving grade that passes under the Capital Beltway before cresting Franconia Hill.

"I could stand on our back porch and watch the Santa Train's diesels roaring as its engineer poured on the coal—as the old steam engine railroaders would say—to get a good run at the hill," Dale Latham recounted in one of our telephone conversations. "It was an amazing sight—the longest passenger train I ever got to see. A big blue and gray streak, since all of the cars were RF&P coaches. And since they ran two or three per day, the Santa Trains became something I really enjoyed watching."[93]

The enjoyment wasn't solely confined to the train's riders. The *Rail-O-Gram*, always abreast of the lives of the RF&P's family of employees, noted in 1967 that a former company official, trainmaster J.W. Garrett, had driven all the way from Kentucky to be in Alexandria just for the occasion.[94]

Gene Luck saw to it that even though J.C. Penney did not have a Snow Queen, as did Miller & Rhoads, it did have entertainment for the children. When the empty train left Richmond's Broad Street Station at 6:00 a.m. for its "deadhead" move (ferrying it to Alexandria for use that day), aboard was Charlie Wakefield with his accordion. There were also clowns and other entertainers.

In later years, as the crowds grew and some of the comfortable blue and gray 500-series cars began to show their age mechanically despite the best efforts of the RF&P shops, Luck sought out additional equipment to fill in for them. A photo showing Santa preparing to board an Alexandria train at

Santa prepares to board the RF&P/J.C. Penney Santa Train at Newington, Virginia, in this 1963 scene. *William E. Griffin Private Collection.*

Newington evidences not only the RF&P sleeping car "Byrd Island" and a blue and yellow coach lettered for the Chesapeake & Ohio Railroad but also three cars belonging to Richmond's Old Dominion Chapter (ODC) of the National Railway Historical Society (NRHS).

Gene Luck's long-standing personal affinity for railroads, going back to his youth in Selma, Alabama, led to friendships with members of this group of dedicated rail enthusiasts. The ODC made preservation of the artifacts and implements of America's great railroad legacy its mission. As such, it had assembled a collection of vintage passenger cars, donated or sold to them, by railroads that deemed these once magnificent treasures to be surplus. With grit, determination and a lot of time and money, the ODC lovingly restored these gems to a level of use that made them railworthy. Leasing them not only made sense for the RF&P, but it also generated funds for the chapter to keep the cars in good repair.

Beginning in 1965, car 1506, which had proudly served the Norfolk & Western Railway before its retirement and ultimate donation to the ODC, began rolling again on RF&P special trains. Still stunning in the N&W's Tuscan red paint and gold lettering, it was joined by two of the chapter's other vintage treasures—McGirth and Dinwiddie County. Members of the ODC—such as Jack Stith, Bill Stratton, Carlton McKenney, Charles Curley Jr. and scores of others too numerous to mention—volunteered their time to man the equipment. According to their monthly publication, the *Highball*, aside from serving coffee and doughnuts to the trains' crews, Stratton administered first aid to an RF&P employee who'd sustained a slight cut from a sliding door and used his coach key to free two young girls who had locked themselves in the ladies' room of one coach.[95]

Not all J.C. Penney stores were located in large or medium-sized cities however. When the chain opted to sponsor a Santa Claus train in 1960 for its outlet in Petersburg, Virginia, a thriving tobacco and manufacturing center twenty miles south of Richmond, it joined with competitor W.T. Grant Company. Except for trains that connected with the Norfolk & Western Railway along the shore of the Appomattox River at the N&W's beautiful columned station in Olde Towne, the Atlantic Coast Line Railroad (ACL) called on Greater Petersburg at a modern-designed, recently completed station in Ettrick, in adjoining Chesterfield County. Located on a line that merely skirted the western edges of Petersburg before crossing a tall steel bridge over the Appomattox River, the Ettrick station sits on the fringe of the campus of Virginia State University. The depot there, also convenient to the neighboring city of Colonial Heights, was blessed with acres of available parking, making it an inviting jumping-off point for the promotion.

Although Gene Luck did not work for the ACL, that railroad's passenger trains were handed off to the RF&P in Richmond for conveyance to Washington's Union Station. The RF&P also took over ACL's freight trains, operating them to Potomac Yard in Alexandria, for forwarding to markets in the Northeast. The two railroads worked together, but the sparse information available about the Ettrick Santa Train affords us very little history about it other than operating dates, its sponsors and a few images and clippings from the *Progress-Index* from Petersburg, Virginia.

Still, Luck's unmistakable fingerprints clearly appear. Ann Blankenship of Chester, Virginia, was kind enough to provide us with sufficient data to conclude that the Petersburg Santa Train consisted of twenty cars. Whether those were the same RF&P coaches or those of host railroad ACL could not be determined. ACL (and rival Seaboard Air Line Railroad) had an immense investment in passenger cars and locomotives with which to equip its vast fleet of Florida streamliners, such as the East and West Coast Champions. ACL's primary passenger equipment shops were located only one hundred miles away in Rocky Mount, North Carolina.

In keeping with the very successful formula that had been used for other Luck-designed Santa Specials, tickets only were available at Penney and Grant locations. The Petersburg train also had clowns and a Snow Queen.

According to the following day's issue of the *Progress-Index*, one railroad employee said he'd never seen anything like it. An hour prior to departure, the area was a sea of automobiles, and to add to the spirit of the season, the cheerleading squad from Colonial Heights High School shouted out greetings to arriving passengers. The cheerleaders were clad in the school's colors, coincidentally, Santa colors—red and white.[96]

Unlike the original Cox Santa Special that operated from Ashland to and through Richmond's Broad Street Station nonstop (about the same distance away as Ettrick), the ACL instead stopped the train at a point on the railroad in South Richmond, just north of Falling Creek. This was where the railroad's century-old main line tracks to downtown—now a lesser-used, mostly industrial branch—diverged from a route that carried the bulk of the ACL's freight and the entirety of its passenger trains across the James River to Broad Street Station and Acca Yard. The diesel locomotives simply swapped ends of the train when they returned to Ettrick.

A SANTA SPECIAL!

How About A Real TRAIN RIDE!

And See SANTA Too:

SATURDAY DEC. 10 – 10 A. M.

- Leave Atlantic Coast Line Station, Ettrick, on a 20-car train pulled by diesels. We'll be back by 12 o'clock. Plenty of parking available at station.
- Santa, clowns and musicians will be with you on this ride. Talk to Santa–eat candy and sing carols and laugh at the clowns.
- Get your tickets at Grants or Penneys for 50c. You must have one to board the train. Only 1000 tickets to sell, so be early.
- Tickets for Tots, Parents–even Grandparents. Each child or group must have an adult with them.

• Jointly sponsored by–

GRANTS — PENNEY'S

The first Ettrick/Petersburg Santa Special, sponsored by J.C. Penney, W.T. Grant and the Atlantic Coast Line Railroad, 1960. *Courtesy Library of Virginia.*

While the managers of Penney and Grant jointly proclaimed the Santa Claus Special a huge success, carrying some 1,100 persons, in ensuing years, Grant declined to renew its sponsorship.

There are always those who step forward to lend a hand for the good of the community, and in that respect, the Greater Petersburg area had no better friend in 1961 than Ettrick American Legion Post 136. That the Santa Claus Special operated beyond its initial season is due in large part to the men and women associated with that organization. The train not only survived but also flourished.

The following year, the train took on a life of its own. Post 136 willingly shouldered the job of promoting the Santa Claus Special, paying for advertising touting a choice of two trains—one at 10:00 a.m., another at 2:00 p.m. The ads went on to mention that one could "talk to Santa, eat candy, drink pop, sample bread loafs [*sic*], free gifts. The works to entertain you."[97]

There were also a number of attractive young ladies—Santa's elves. "There were two or three elves assigned to each car," Annabel Woodriff Newton said in a phone interview. "We wore tights, a white turtleneck and a red skirt that our mothers made for us. We were supposed to watch the children and give out candy canes. Everyone was so excited when Santa came through each car to see everyone!"

Mrs. Newton—at the time, a Petersburg High School student who later attended Matoaca High—pretty much summed up the community spirit that saved the train. "My dad, Bill Woodriff, got me interested in doing it—not for pay, but just to have a good time at Christmas. I and other high school students were chosen to be a part of the excursions since many of the dads of the young people were members of the local American Legion Post 136 in Ettrick. It was our way of giving back to the community."[98]

The outreach of the American Legion post was even apparent from the locations where tickets could be purchased: J.C. Penney, Billy Gill's Used Car Lot and Wise Way Food Stores. The community came together behind something they believed in and, at least for a couple years more, saved the Santa Claus Special.

Mrs. Edythe Gill, now ninety-three, who retired in 1982 after forty-four years as an educator in Chesterfield County, spent most of her career as a third grade teacher at Ettrick Elementary School. Mrs. Gill's late husband, Billy, as well as his brother, Herbert Gill, and his wife, Olive, were charter members of Post 136.

Many of her former students were elves aboard the 1961–63 Santa Claus Specials. Annabel Woodriff Newton and Linda Burton Waggerspeck are two former students with whom she keeps in touch. "Both of their mothers made their elf outfits," Mrs. Gill said.[99]

While she did not personally ride the train, her interaction with the Atlantic Coast Line Railroad officials resulted in the teaching of a "transportation" unit at her school. "About sixty students were treated to a train trip to Broad Street Station, given a tour and a picnic on the grounds. For many, it was their first train trip. The same for the Santa Claus Special," she added.[100]

Many people recall riding the train. None, however, were able to provide pictures. It was only a few days before our deadline loomed that Mrs. Gill informed us that after a photo search by members of Post 136 and an appeal to longtime residents of Ettrick and Petersburg for images, no memorabilia could be found. She explained that the likelihood of finding anything was not very promising because much of the organization's archives had been lost in a fire some years ago.

Annabel Woodriff Newton commented, "We couldn't understand why they stopped. It [the Santa Train] was a wonderful thing."[101]

An ad appeared in the Friday, November 22, 1963 *Progress-Index*, announcing what would inevitably be the final Santa Claus Special to be operated by the Petersburg J.C. Penney store and Ettrick American Legion Post 136. In retrospect, other events of that sad day surely overshadowed news of the train—the date of the assassination of President John F. Kennedy. Additionally, the date of the final Santa Claus Special would fall on the anniversary of another date that was haunting yet dear to Americans—December 7.

CHAPTER 14

WHAT ARE THE CHANCES?

Incredibly, but for a momentary lapse of memory resulting in an inadvertent slip of the tongue, one obscure Virginia Santa Train would have been overlooked entirely in the production of this book. When one of the interviewees for this book, a former Miller & Rhoads Snow Queen, thought that she and Santa had been put into a limousine at the downtown Richmond store and driven to the small Piedmont Virginia community of Zion Crossroads—not Ashland, as was the normal routine for the trains that the store operated out of Broad Street Station over the Richmond, Fredericksburg & Potomac Railroad—we were immediately thrown into a quandary. Upon further reflection, she assured us that she had not been taken to Doswell or Elmont or Taylorsville; she had gone to Zion Crossroads. We were stumped. She further claimed that the train on which she served as Santa's Snow Queen that night returned to Broad Street Station.

Our confusion stemmed from the fact that you can't get from Zion Crossroads to Broad Street Station. We began questioning our own sanity and why we had agreed to write this book. We felt fairly comfortable with our collective knowledge of railroading in Virginia, but we wondered whether there had been some Santa Train operating in the woods of Fluvanna or Louisa County of which no one but this Snow Queen was aware and on tracks that no longer existed.

Zion Crossroads today consists of a few isolated homes, a couple of service stations and a post office near the offramp of an interchange on

Interstate 64, west of Richmond. The only marked difference in today's town and that of the late 1950s is that Interstate 64 exists. The service station might have been remodeled and the price of postage increased, but everything else is the same—almost.

Until the mid-1960s, there was a little-used, twenty-five-mile-per-hour freight branch line of the Chesapeake & Ohio that passed through Zion Crossroads, but it did not stop. The railroad was abandoned, and the track was removed. No Santa Train had ever operated over those rails to our knowledge, but to make sure, we contacted a former co-worker, a retired railroader living in Florida, who was born and raised there.

Not surprisingly, he'd never heard of a Santa Train operating through or anywhere near Zion Crossroads. Possibly the lady meant that she'd been driven through Zion Crossroads on her way to…well, where would she have been going? We had discovered that Miller & Rhoads operated Santa Trains in Roanoke and Lynchburg, and we were fully investigating those towns for any leads. We'd found out about Cox department store in Ashland. Doug Riddell has lived there for the past two years and had even dined at the Iron Horse Restaurant at a table on what had been the sales floor of the store, unaware of the fact that, in that particular place years ago, women had been trying on clothes at a point behind the bar.

There was one possibility: Miller & Rhoads had a downtown Charlottesville store and, in 1965, had opened up a suburban location near the University of Virginia in the Barracks Road Shopping Center.[102] Maybe this particular Snow Queen had seen a highway sign indicating that the car in which she was riding was passing through Zion Crossroads. Only two railroads ran through Charlottesville: the Southern Railway and the Chesapeake & Ohio. If this was another one of Gene Luck's Santa Trains for Miller & Rhoads, it would have boarded Santa and the Snow Queen at some point about twenty miles from Thomas Jefferson's town: Orange, on the Southern Railway, or Gordonsville, on the C&O.

With this in mind, we made a frantic call to Bill Schafer, who like Doug Riddell, had just retired from the railroad. The Southern Railway System had originally hired Schafer, a career executive for Norfolk Southern Corporation. He'd helped to put out its employee magazine, *Ties*. He was a walking encyclopedia regarding the Southern.

"Funny you should mention it," Schafer laughed when we called him at his home in Virginia Beach. "Back in December 1967, I was riding our train Number 36, in a private car attached to the rear. It was the last day of operation. We were routed into the siding as we approached

Charlottesville and suddenly this unscheduled train went flying by—two E8s [diesel-electric passenger locomotive] and about a dozen old heavyweight cars. The dispatcher called on the radio to inform us that it was a Santa Claus Special that would be unloading passengers at the Charlottesville station. It's the only Santa Train I ever remember seeing on the Southern. The private car I was riding belonged to Walter Loftin. Call him."[103]

We quickly scribbled down the number and made the call. "Yes," Loftin said. "It was December 2, 1967—the final run of Number 36. They operated three round trips to Orange from Charlottesville. To my knowledge, they had never done it before and, as far as I know, never did it again."[104]

Some months later, on May 16, in the preservation archives offices of Norfolk Southern's headquarters in Norfolk, Virginia, coauthor Donna Strother Deekens was going through bound editions of *Ties* and found the 1967 collection. "You're not going to believe what I found; the 1967 Santa Claus Special from Charlottesville to Orange, Virginia," she read, as she flipped the page.

"Was it sponsored by Miller & Rhoads?" Doug Riddell asked.

"No, Doug, it was a promotion by the retail merchants of Downtown Charlottesville," Donna nodded. "Several pages and lots of pictures."

"So, is our Snow Queen pictured in the article?"

"Oh, there's a Snow Queen, but she's identified as a former 'Miss Charlottesville,'" she read on.

Although Miller & Rhoads went out of business almost a quarter century ago, its employees still gather formally and informally. When you've shared as much as they have and have been as close as they were, I would imagine that it's difficult, if not impossible, to sever relationships so securely bound. In meeting with a group of them to do research, the story of the Charlottesville train arose. "Jack West. You remember Jack West, don't you?" a voice was heard to say. "He was the store manager in Charlottesville during most of the 1960s. He'll know, I'm sure."

"Yes, I vividly recall the Charlottesville Santa Train," John W. "Jack" West said at the Miller & Rhoads retirees' luncheon. He had been the manager of the Charlottesville Miller & Rhoads downtown store from 1964 to 1969. He was able to give us some of the details of the Charlottesville to Orange specials sponsored by the Southern Railway and the Charlottesville Downtown Retail Merchants—or Downtown Charlottesville, Incorporated, as it was called then. "Although it wasn't

Snow is appropriate at Christmas as passengers board the Downtown Charlottesville Incorporated Santa Special on one day only, December 2, 1967. *Courtesy Norfolk Southern Corp.*

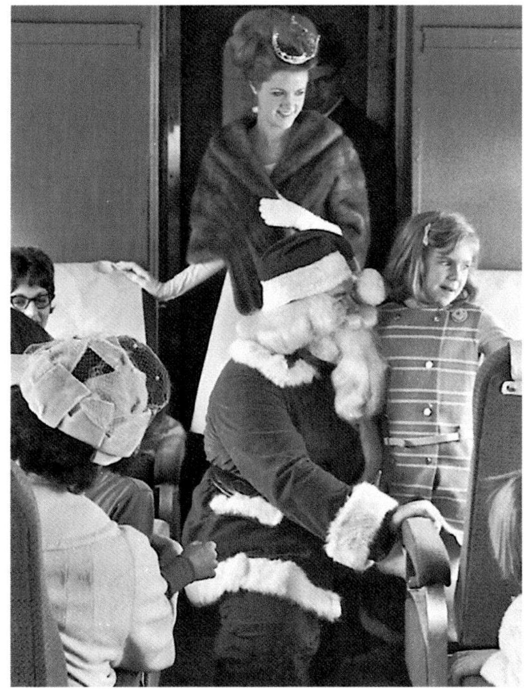

A young girl meets Santa aboard the Santa Special, sponsored by the Southern Railway and Downtown Charlottesville Incorporated, 1967. *Courtesy Norfolk Southern Corp.*

ours, since I was the store manager at Miller & Rhoads, I accepted an invitation to be a 'helper,' going up and down the aisle to manage the children, even though there were parents aboard."

"It was a long time ago, but it was special," agreed Jack West.[105]

So yes, Virginia, there was another Santa Claus Train. It ran for only one day and made three round trips. The odds were incalculably small that it would be discovered, and it was even less likely that someone would be around to tell us about it.

So at this point, we were left to ponder the fate of the Miller & Rhoads Snow Queen who was taken to Zion Crossroads. A return phone call from her a couple of days later solved the mystery.

"Doswell, not Zion Crossroads. Yes, I was thinking about it, and I'm sure now it was Doswell," exclaimed Nancy Pace Newton.[106]

Community involvement by a merchant group, especially in a city the size of Fredericksburg, Virginia, can also play an important role. Midway between Richmond and Washington, D.C., Fredericksburg has had the best of both worlds for a long time. It's been able to benefit from the cultural and economic pluses of being a commutable suburb of the nation's capital yet retains its charm as a small riverfront city whose roots reach back to George Washington. Our first president learned his trade as a surveyor while living at his brother's estate across the Rappahannock

Santa greets the arrival of his Southern Railway "special train" at Orange, Virginia, in four inches of snow on December 2, 1967. *Courtesy Norfolk Southern Corp.*

at Ferry Farm (coauthor Donna Strother Deekens says this was the property initially known as the "Strother Farm" and was sold to George Washington's father by her early ancestors).

Absent from the city of Fredericksburg was a large department store of its own to act as a benefactor when the RF&P began operating Santa Trains from Richmond in 1957, but the Fredericksburg Retail Merchants Association formulated a plan. They hoped that when the Christmas season of 1958 came around, they would be able to host their own Santa Claus Special.

Like Alexandria's, Fredericksburg's economy benefited from comparatively stable and well-paying public sector jobs from Northern Virginia as well as the large Dahlgren Proving Grounds to the east on the banks of the Potomac. For all the years from the inception of their Santa Train until all of the trains ended in 1971, the residents of the city and neighboring counties filled their Santa Trains to overflowing with little more than an announcement appearing in the *Fredericksburg Freelance-Star*.

The *Highball*, the monthly publication of Richmond's Old Dominion Chapter of the National Railway Historical Society, records that on Saturday, December 7, 1966, two round trips were made between Fredericksburg and Quantico, employing three of the chapter's restored vintage rail cars.[107]

Lee Milstead, a Fredericksburg native who would go on to become a member of the fraternity of that high calling to don a red suit and white beard at Christmas to bring smiles to the faces of the young and young at heart, remembers clamoring aboard the Santa trains for his round trip to Quantico from the late 1950s into the 1960s. "I was really little, and I only remember a few flashbacks," he reported in a phone interview. "I definitely remember boarding the train in downtown Fredericksburg, and I recall sitting on the left-hand side of the train car with my mother. Santa came through the cars and greeted all the children. I remember there were clowns and musicians, as well, and we all received a gift of some kind—a candy cane, I think."[108]

Even community support could not prevent the demise of the Santa Trains. Eventually, the wheels stopped rolling. They would return, however, looking a bit different than when Gene Luck was aboard, leaning out the top of a Dutch door, scanning the platform of one of his Santa Trains. He probably felt the same then as Lee Milstead has ever since he rode his first Santa Train and visited the real Santa in Santaland at Miller & Rhoads in downtown Richmond, living the magic.

CHAPTER 15

BLESSED BE THE CROSSTIES THAT BIND

Railroads built America. The names of few if any major population centers come to mind that are not connected by a rail. Communities sprung up along routes as they were built. Most were designed to connect trading posts and centers of commerce to one another or to ports where goods and people could continue their journeys by waterways. Most meandered along riverbanks when crossing hills and mountains to take advantage of the easiest grades over which to pull heavy trains. It made no difference that this increased distances from one point to another. At the time, other than boats and barges, the railroad's only competition outside large urban areas was largely unpaved roads—two ruts in the ground subject to adverse weather.

Citizens of towns that might otherwise have been left isolated enticed railroad builders to revise their maps or construct dedicated branch lines so they could be connected. Railroads were lured by offers that included extensive swaths of land on which to lay their network of ballast, crossties and rails, with ample space left over for development.

In return, the railroads pledged service to their patrons. Rail companies were local. Everyone knew the telegraph operator or stationmaster as well as they did the town doctor or minister. The conductor and engineer of the daily train to Timbuktu knew the name of every man, woman and child. There was a thrill at hearing the whistle of a train approaching a small town because it meant excitement. It meant commerce and prosperity were about to pull into the depot.

Sedley, a small community nestled in the vast green peanut fields of Southampton County, Virginia, was one such town. The Virginian Railway cut through its center, although, as in the case of the chicken or the egg, one has to wonder if the town did not evolve around the railroad. Wealthy industrialist Henry Huttleston Rogers built the Virginian with his own money long after competitors, Norfolk & Western and Chesapeake & Ohio, were already hauling coal from the hills and hollows of West Virginia to the port cities of Hampton Roads. The C&O arrived in Newport News on the north side of the James River, whereas the N&W clung to Virginia's south side, crossing the Great Dismal Swamp before entering Norfolk.

Rogers would benefit from hindsight—the mistakes of his competitors. By employing modern technology and engineering, he was able to construct a route characterized by gentler grades that resulted in being able to haul coal more efficiently. He wasn't averse to general freight carriage, but the Virginian's focus was on coal. Because it generally avoided large population centers, the market and the demand for passenger service were sparse.

Largely living in the shadow of the nearby city of Franklin, which benefited from the presence of a prominent manufacturing concern, Sedley was a pleasant place to live, work and worship in peace and tranquility. Its beautiful homes were byproducts of timber and agriculture—most specifically peanuts. The small town's Woman's and Ruritan Clubs were both active and prominent.

Virginian locomotive 215 was used in Virginia passenger service, including trains that brought Santa to Sedley, circa 1950. *Courtesy Sargeant Memorial Collection, Norfolk Public Library.*

This watercolor, painted by the late Mrs. Ann Creasey, shows the now demolished Virginian Railway depot in Sedley, Virginia, circa 1950. *James A. Creasy Private Collection.*

Nancy Cogsdale, who twice served as president of the Sedley Woman's Club, pointed out, "The Woman's Club provided milk routes to the schools and was responsible for Sedley receiving its first streetlights. We were a very active, very civic-minded community for our time."[109]

Few examples of civic pride stand out as clearly as the annual arrival of Santa Claus at Sedley, aboard Virginian Railway passenger train Number 4 The saga, cited in *Extra South*, a book of railroad memories by Newport News newspaper editor and author H. Reid, was well known in the area and rivaled events of all kinds anywhere else in Southampton County.[110]

Thanks to the two local service organizations, the eagerly waited for holiday rite became an opportunity for the citizens of Sedley to share the spirit of the season with those less fortunate than themselves. In doing so, they created a tradition that lives on in the hearts of its residents more than sixty years after the last Santa Train chugged off into the east.

To the people of Sedley, when flyers announced the first coming of Santa aboard a train, word spread throughout the community. The playbill in the window of the Sedley Theatre noted simply: "Saturday, Santa Claus, In Person, 2:30 PM, Cartoon and Comedy Show, Adm. Package of Canned Food."[111]

Illustrator Joe Easley's conception of the arrival of the Virginia passenger train at Sedley, Virginia, delivering Santa Claus, circa 1950. *Courtesy Carsten's Publications.*

"Each child was asked to bring a canned good for [his or her] admission price," remembered Patricia Duck Carter, whose father, P.O. Duck, owned and operated the theater with assistance of her mother, Hattie. (Since Mrs. P.O. Duck worked at the post office, she was affectionately known as Mrs. Post Office Duck.) Members of the Sedley Woman's Club made up gift baskets for the underprivileged families in the area. "One year, 1951, the ladies asked for donations of clothing, in addition to canned goods, for the Korean War effort," she added.[112]

Viewing the black-and-white 8mm home movies of the first Sedley Santa Train, you'd think that you were looking at a huge celebration in a large city. The edges of the narrow street that crossed the tracks were jammed with automobiles as far as the eye could see. Throngs of youngsters—fathers with their sons and daughters clasping hands, mothers with babies in their arms—walked to the station to await the arrival of Number 4 at 2:30 p.m.

Outside town, at a location identified in the Virginian Railway employee timetable as Morgan, the eastbound passenger train had halted momentarily so that engine Number 215's thirst for water and hunger for coal could be satisfied. While one crew member struggled to position the balky coal chute to spill its bounty into the open tender car that was attached to the steam locomotive, another shielded himself from the torrent of water that spilled into the tender's tank compartment.

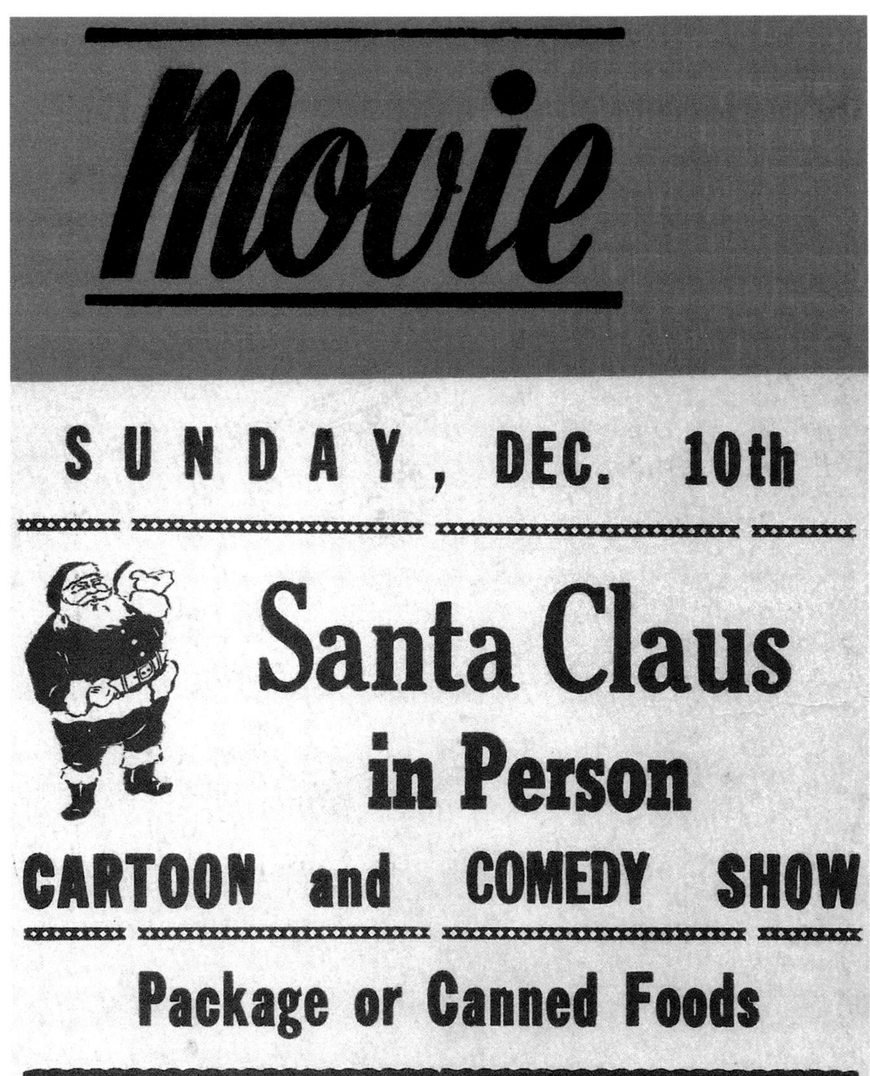

Santa's appearance at the Sedley Theatre, announced in a poster, was distributed community-wide, circa 1950. *P.O. Duck Private Collection, courtesy Patricia Duck Carter.*

The Morgan coal chute near Sedley, where Woman's Club ladies decorated the engine and Santa boarded, circa 1950. *H.B. and Anne Bryant Private Collection.*

The ladies of the Sedley Woman's Club were given charge of the standing train at Morgan, turning the grimy, greasy machine into Santa's sleigh. "During the stop, the locomotive was decorated with holly, and a huge wreath was placed on the front," both Nancy Cogsdale and Patricia Duck Carter recalled.[113]

Checking his watch, the conductor stood on the ground, mindful that they had only a few minutes to perform their duties and begin moving again before it would become necessary to send out the train's flagman to protect it from being overtaken by a following train.

Morgan was not a location where Virginian trains normally boarded passengers; but that day, there would be an exception. And this traveler would not be required to produce a ticket or a pass. Everyone knew who he was, and it is doubtful that anyone hoping to get something better than a lump of coal in their Christmas stocking would deny this gentleman a seat on their train. It was Santa Claus.

"We had a wonderful Santa," Mrs. Cogsdale told us. "Elvin Whitley. He was a local resident. He'd meet with each child while all waiting children were entertained by the theater's owner, P.O. Duck, who showed cartoons. Santa was genuinely affectionate with the children and laughed with them."[114]

Santa would only be traveling the mile or so to the Sedley depot. He'd most likely simply stand in the vestibule of the first coach until the conductor stopped the train, opened the door and then permitted him to detrain.

With a couple of toots from the 215's whistle, the flagman hopped aboard the rear of the train and waved his lantern up and down to let the engineer know he was aboard, and with a long hiss, the driving wheels of the steam locomotive began to turn. With each revolution, it moved faster, until the little steam engine had the three cars in its charge, speeding down the track toward Sedley.

Waiting for the train, Mrs. Joan Hundley Powell recalled a fond memory: "My parents said, as the train approached, for us children to be sure and turn our heads or we'd get those cinders in our eyes, since the train would throw out so much stuff from the rails." She noted that it was particularly good advice, since her grandfather Herbert Chappell had worked at the train depot.[115]

The engineer no sooner reached the train's cruising speed than he began reducing the throttle and applying the brakes, preparing for the station stop. Santa waved to the crowd as Number 4 pulled in. The train's conductor placed a step box on the ground below the coach car's bottom step to allow

Santa Claus hugs two Sedley, Virginia youngsters after arriving in town on the Virginian Railway steam passenger train, circa 1951. *June Hundley Dunlow Private Collection.*

passengers to detrain and board with greater ease, but jolly ol' Saint Nick came bounding down the steps, shaking hands with the conductor and triumphantly waving both hands high above his head as a crush of young boys and girls greeted him. Passengers getting on and off the train at Sedley were caught up in the merriment as Santa and the children moved back from the train. Within a minute or so after it had stopped, Number 4 began to move east. This day was no different than any other, in that respect. Norfolk was not that far ahead, and everything had to be done to see that the eastbound Virginian passenger train that day was on time, as it was expected to be on any day.

Santa appeared as happy to be in Sedley as the children of the town were to see him. Jovial and light on his feet, he stopped to peek into the windows of automobiles that had double parked in the middle of the dirt road that ran north of the tracks and made his way past Rogers Park to the Sedley Theatre. Everyone wanted to see Santa Claus, even those too young or physically unable to do so, so the jolly ol' elf stopped to greet them.

Although she was only three, too young to remember the first year, Patricia Duck Carter had a front-row seat for the last four years of the Santa Special. "It was a grand and glorious event."[116]

Wesley Wills, a longtime resident of Franklin and active at age eighty-eight, agrees that it was a "truly wonderful thing" that folks who were around at the time still talk about today. "Our oldest son, Ellis, was born in 1951, and we made it an annual event to take him every year when the Santa Train came to Sedley in the 1950s."[117]

Typical of early December in southeastern Virginia, where the warmth of the nearby Atlantic Ocean results in a mist that envelopes small Southampton County towns like Sedley, in the old 8mm films, it appeared gray and cloudy. But the looks on the faces of the young kids lit up the town. The parade of people stopped at the park momentarily, as a group of children succeeded in getting Santa to hold hands and join them as they danced in circles. Finally breaking away, everyone filed into the Sedley Theatre for cartoons, dropping off their canned goods—their admission price—as they passed through the door.

"My husband remembers he got gifts of an apple or an orange and candy," added Donna Neal Turner, whose husband, Sedley native Tommy Turner, and sister-in-law, Becky Turner Edwards, both rode the Santa Claus Special in the late 1940s and into the 1950s.[118]

As the light faded, ministers from the town's churches began to gather around a cedar tree that was decorated in Rogers Park, joined by parents waiting for their sons and daughters to exit the theater. In a scene worthy of a Christmas card, they began to carol the songs of the season.

The Santa Train stopped at Sedley every year from 1948 until Christmas 1955. On January 29, 1956, however, the Virginian Railway ran its final passenger trains, Numbers 3 and 4, between Roanoke and Norfolk.

Sedley Theatre entrance, circa 1950. As was that era's custom, there were separate entrances for blacks and whites. *H.B. and Anne Bryant Private Collection.*

Not to be deterred, the Woman's Club of Sedley, along with the town's Ruritan Club, arranged for Santa to make his grand entrance in a number of ways in subsequent years, but none was as unforgettable as when he stepped off the Virginian Railway train and onto the platform of the town's depot.

In the ensuing days, steam locomotive Number 215 and other Virginian locomotives were eased into siding tracks at the railroad's large terminals. In their places were big yellow and black diesel-electric locomotives built by Fairbanks-Morse in Beloit, Wisconsin. In 1959, rival Norfolk & Western acquired the Virginian Railway, and within a few years, the tracks were abandoned and taken up, sadly. Since governments tend to view railroads as cash cows, tracks and structures that aren't essential for operations are customarily razed to avoid paying the tax man. Little of the Virginian Railway remains today except in the hearts and memories of people who were touched by it.

On at least one cold winter day around Christmas, the residents of the town of Sedley, Virginia, gather at Rogers Park. A fire truck arrives, its siren and horn blaring, its lights spinning and flashing. Santa steps down and greets the adults, children and grandchildren who are there to meet him, and some are the same who were present those many years ago to greet the Santa Train and accompany the special visitor to the Sedley Theatre. Many of the buildings that once composed a vibrant business district are gone. Some, like the theater, have been remodeled and now serve other purposes.

As the festivities go on, however, one is tempted to look down the railroad right of way, now a grown-over utility easement, below which flows fresh water from Lake Gaston to the cities in Tidewater Virginia. You can almost hear that whistle resonate across the fields of peanuts, where startled deer stop their feeding for a brief moment to reassure themselves that they are alone. You can imagine the glowing headlight of eastbound train Number 4, with smoke escaping from the stack of engine Number 215. But it is only in memories that Santa will step down from the coach of the Sedley Santa Train.

June Hundley Dunlow, a member of the Sedley Woman's Club and daughter of the late Mary D. Hundley, who also served the club as a member for many years, has a special memento of the Sedley Santa Train. It is a poem written by her mother:[119]

Nostalgia Trip

It's the second week in December
And the air is feeling crisp.
All of Sedley is a bustle
For a real Nostalgia Trip.

The park is full of people
A thousand, I would say
From all surrounding communities
For this eventful day.

Children are running here and there
Excited as can be!
Old Santa's arrival on the train
Is what they want to see.

I hear the whistle from afar
The engine is decked with holly.
Oh, there's Santa at the door
And he's really acting jolly!

Grabbing his hands, away they go
With cries of admiration,
Laughing and talking to and fro
The theater is their destination.

Canned good is the price for a ticket
For those less fortunate, they say,
To be packed in baskets later on
And delivered for Christmas Day.

With Santa's chair at center stage
And his elves on either side,
The children state their wishes and say
They've been good!—with pride.

A gift from Santa's bag is given
And free cartoons to view,

But the party isn't over yet
There are still things left to do.

Back to the Park they make their way
And gather around the tree.
A switch is thrown and lights come on.
Oh, what sight to see!

Birth of the Christ Child, Rev. Coney says
This is the real reason,
And voices of the Community Choir
Ring out with carols of the season.

God bless the women of the Woman's Club.
God bless the Ruritans, too.
For without their love and caring
This event wouldn't be true.

Mary D. Hundley
1986

Farther west, the Isle of Wight town of Zuni sits beside the former Norfolk & Western Railway tracks that date back to the Civil War. The main line of today's Norfolk Southern, trains still speed through the town, as they always have. Only the daily N&W local passenger trains stopped there (and at just about every other small station on the line). They were the bane of travelers who wished to get somewhere quickly because they barely had time to get up to speed before their next stop. Local passenger trains were slow.

If you lived in Zuni in 1951, you were thankful for locals 23 and 24, though, because on a day near Christmas, Santa would step down from one of the day coaches and walk downhill from the depot, carefully cross U.S. Route 460 and enter the quaint country store.

Joe Brinkley Jr., who was about five or six years old at the time, remembered the event: "About fifty people were gathered at the store—many on the front porch—to watch for Santa's arrival. My grandfather was with me and had actually anticipated Santa's arrival days before. It was so very exciting. Once Santa got through the crowd into the store, the children would line up to visit with him. He spent quite a while there."

Joe Brinkley remembers in his watercolor creation the N&W passenger train stopping in Zuni, Virginia, delivering Santa, circa 1947. *Joe Brinkley Private Collection.*

For children living in such rural settings, this was Christmas. In the days before tropical fruits were available year round, getting an orange was a rare treat. "I remember each of us was given a cellophane bag with oranges, apples, nuts and candy," Brinkley recalled. "It is one of the dearest memories of my childhood."[120]

Brinkley was so moved by this recollection that he used watercolors to illustrate the scene. It was reproduced as a postcard as part of Zuni's history.

The coal that flows via trains through Zuni, and at one time moved through Sedley, originated in the mines of Appalachia. Visiting there during his 1960 presidential campaign, John F. Kennedy was moved to comment afterward that he had no idea poverty of such magnitude existed in the United States. The Clinchfield Railroad, a predecessor unit of CSX, served an extensive network of mines in an area where the states of Virginia, Tennessee and Kentucky merge—one of the country's most economically disadvantaged regions.

A benevolent gesture by a small group of merchants in Kingsport, Tennessee, in 1943 has evolved into a nationally known holiday tradition, thanks to media exposure from the likes of the late correspondent Charles

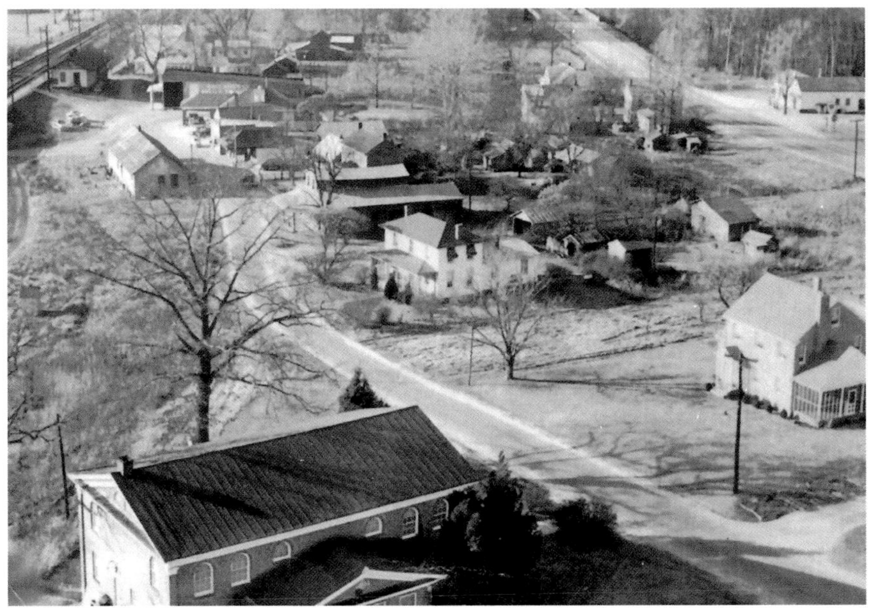

Zuni, Virginia, depicted on a postcard, with N&W depot in the upper left, circa 1950. *Judson Bowden photograph, collection of W.C. Andrews III, courtesy Jane March.*

Kuralt, who covered the Santa Train during one of his "On the Road" reports for CBS. The *New York Times* also helped make America aware of this outpouring of charity by printing a front-page spread. Books have been written and films produced that have told this endearing story. Celebrities, many from circumstances that often mirror those of the young faces portrayed with outstretched hands, all come away following their participation, touched by the experience.

CSX Transportation has continued the tradition started by the Clinchfield Railroad, donating the use of its equipment and crews for the train that usually leaves Pikeville, Kentucky, on its 110-mile journey to Kingsport, arriving there in time for the city's annual Christmas parade. The train was originally steam powered, and for its fiftieth anniversary, the Union Pacific Challenger—the largest operating steam locomotive in America, almost identical to ones used to haul coal by the Clinchfield—powered the Santa Train.

Santa and his helpers always are on the open platform at the rear of the train. Along the way, the train slows down so that he can gently toss gifts to families who appear at isolated points beside the tracks. He also hands out

CSX carries on the 1943 Santa Special tradition, serving the people along the original Clinchfield Railroad, as depicted in this Ron Flannery illustration. *Courtesy CSX.*

packages to those at scheduled stops the Santa Train makes. In total, fully fifteen tons of donated goods are distributed.

Santa might have eight tiny reindeer (OK, nine if we include Rudolph), but he has had, and continues to enjoy, the support of thousands of horses—whether steam or diesel—to pull his train: the Santa Claus Special.

CHAPTER 16

HEADIN' HOME FOR THE HOLIDAYS

Having worked for the railroad for thirty-five years, coauthor Doug Riddell knows what its like to be away from his family, traveling at Christmastime. People are either overjoyed at being on their way home, or they're miserably alone in a crowd of strangers.

Doug Riddell and coauthor Donna Strother Deekens had the pleasure of traveling to Raleigh, North Carolina, to continue their research. There, Doug was able to renew an old friendship with former railroader Jim Grem, who served as Santa in his Masonic lodge. Grem took his role to a new level when on one Christmas Eve he began bringing along his Santa suit on the Silver Star, between Raleigh and Richmond, before he retired from the Seaboard Coast Line Railroad/CSX in 1997.

Once business was taken care of, he'd slip into the crew dormitory car and emerge as "Saint Nick." For an hour or so before the train would reach Petersburg, Virginia, "Santa Jim" would roam the train, handing out candy to both kids and adults—candy Grem had purchased at his own expense, which he carried around in ten-pound sacks.

"I'd open the door, and the kids would yell out, 'Here comes Santa Claus!' They'd be two to ten years old. Their eyes would grow big as softballs. But they'd all say, 'Thank you, thank you, thank you!'" the old conductor remembered with a huge smile on his own face.

He'd do the same on the return trip in the evening run to Raleigh, between Petersburg, Virginia, and Wake Forest, North Carolina, where he'd reappear as the train's conductor before concluding his day.

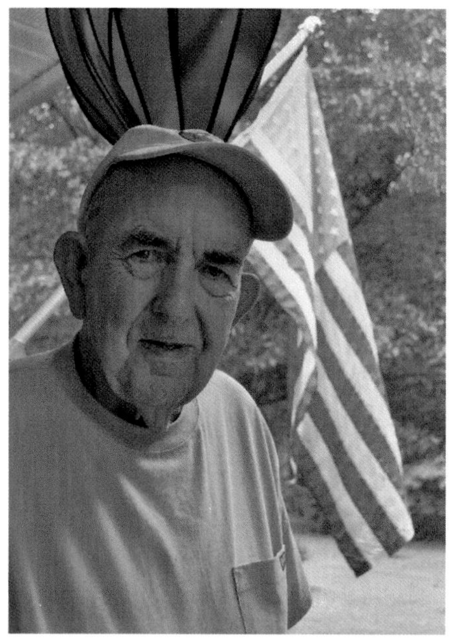

Seaboard Coast Line conductor Jim Grem spent Christmas Eves dressed as Santa aboard the train, distributing candy and good will. *Doug Riddell Private Collection.*

"The candy was always appreciated," Grem laughed. "Sometimes, you could tell if that was the only food someone had enjoyed in a while. You could tell it was a poor family on the train, because they'd be eating their food in their seat—not in the dining car."

Santa Jim was a real life Santa, all year round, it appears. Introduced to a young girl who lived in Murfreesboro, North Carolina, born with one of her eyes out of place on her forehead, Grem worked through the Shriners, who were involved in the Eye Bank. They sponsored the surgery that corrected her condition. According to Grem, she completed school, went on to live a normal life and became an executive with a large soft drink manufacturer in Atlanta, Georgia.

Both the Seaboard Coast Line Railroad and Amtrak commended Jim Grem numerous times for sharing the spirit of Christmas aboard his train, and someone in Georgia also thinks he's sort of special, too, we're sure.[121]

The deeds of Jim Grem bring to mind a poem by Henry C. Walsh:

Santa Claus on the Train[122]
Henry C. Walsh

On a Christmas Eve an emigrant train
Sped on through the blackness of night

And left the pitchy dark in twain
With the gleam of its fierce headlight.

In a crowded car, a noisome place,
Sat a mother and her child;
The woman's face bore want's wan trace,
But the little one only smiled,

And tugged and pulled at her mother's dress,
And her voice had a merry ring,
As she lisped, "Now, mamma, come and guess
What Santa Claus'll bring."

But sadly the mother shook her head,
As she thought of a happier past;
"He never can catch us here," she said.
"The train is going too fast."

"O, mamma, yes, he'll come, I say,
So swift are his little deer,
They run all over the world today;
I'll hang my stocking up here."

She pinned her stocking to the seat,
And closed her tired eyes;
And soon she saw each longed-for sweet
In dreamland's paradise.

On a seat behind the little maid
A rough man sat apart,
But a soft light o'er his features played,
And stole into his heart.

As the cars drew up at a busy town
The rough man left the train,
But scarce had from the steps jumped down
Ere he was back again.

And a great big bundle of Christmas joys
Bulged out from his pocket wide;
He filled the stocking with sweets and toys
He laid by the dreamer's side.

At dawn the little one woke with a shout,
'Twas sweet to hear her glee;
"I knowed that Santa Claus would find me out;
He caught the train you see."

Though some from smiling may scarce refrain,
The child was surely right,
The good St. Nicolas caught the train,
And came aboard that night.

For the saint is fond of masquerade
And may fool the old and wise,
And so he came to the little maid,
In an emigrant's disguise.

And he dresses in many ways because
He wishes no one to know him,
For he never says, "I am Santa Claus,"
But his good deeds always show him.

If you ever caught an Amtrak train at Washington, D.C.'s Union Station and thought you saw Santa at the throttle of a locomotive switching passenger cars at Christmas, there's nothing wrong with your eyes. For many years, engineer Timmy O'Neal would appear as "Santa Timmy," using his lunch break to distribute candy to delighted children in the waiting areas of the boarding concourse.

Amtrak has regularly supported the efforts of the U.S. Marines, providing space near boarding gates and encouraging their own personnel to volunteer collecting donations for the Toys4Tots program. Coauthor Doug Riddell was the engineer for the 1987 Toys4Tots special that ran between Washington, D.C., and Alexandria, Virginia, as part of a media event to promote the very worthy cause.

The Norfolk & Western Railway, however, took the Christmas spirit to heart many years ago, setting up decorative trees in its dining cars and

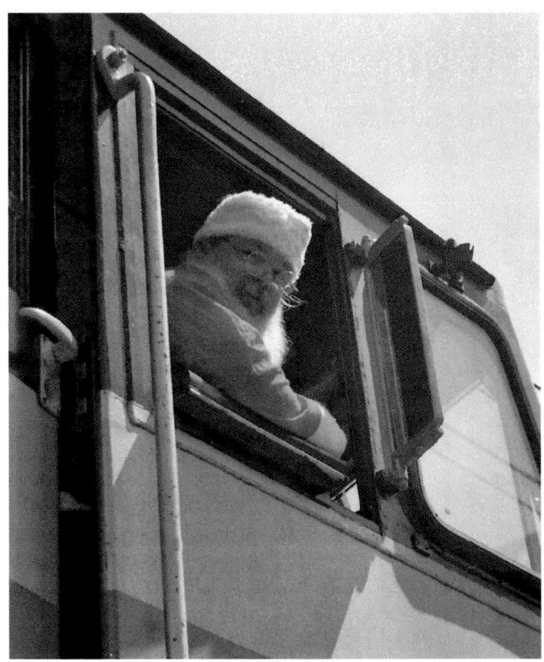

Santa Timmy O'Neal spreads cheer in the cab at Washington Union Station, as well as greets passengers inside the station, 1995. *Doug Riddell Private Collection.*

Amtrak engineer Doug Riddell and wife, Sandy, ready the U.S. Marine Corps' Toys4Tots Christmas special, at Washington, D.C.'s Union Station, 1987. *Doug Riddell Private Collection.*

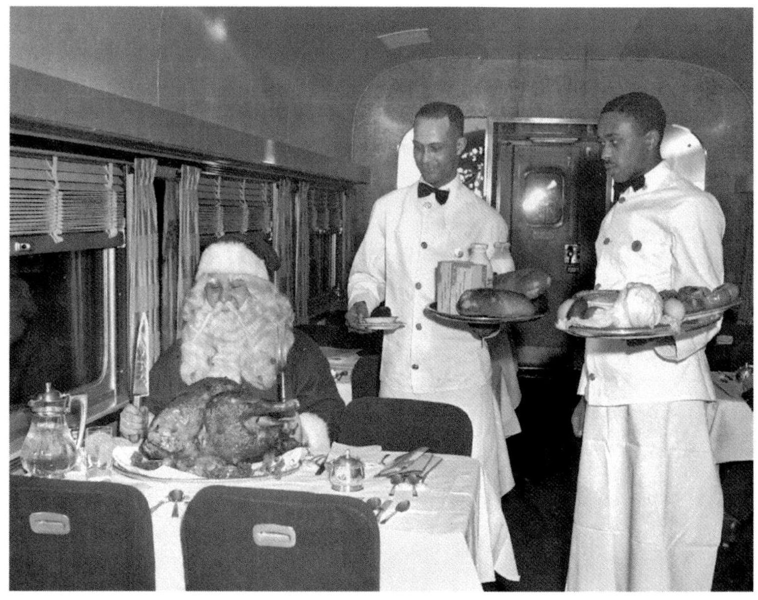

Santa pauses for a delicious N&W dining car meal while en route on his holiday ramble, December 1950. *Courtesy Norfolk Southern Corp.*

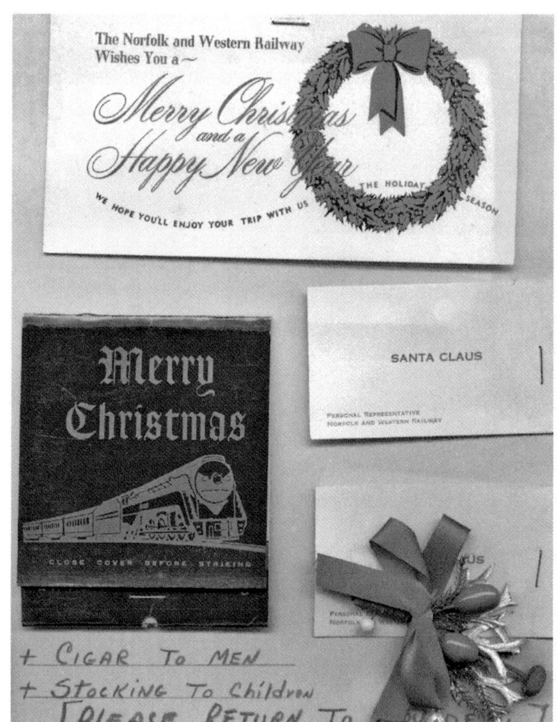

Examples of souvenir items presented to passengers by Santa Claus aboard Norfolk & Western trains, December 1950. *Courtesy Norfolk Southern Corp.*

Santa gifts ladies and children with Christmas stockings and gentlemen with cigars aboard the Norfolk & Western passenger train, December 1950. *Courtesy Norfolk Southern Corp.*

Even though the country had been plunged into the midst of the Great Depression, Santa arrived in Roanoke aboard Norfolk & Western car Number 3 on December 15, 1929. *J.L. Sanders Private Collection.*

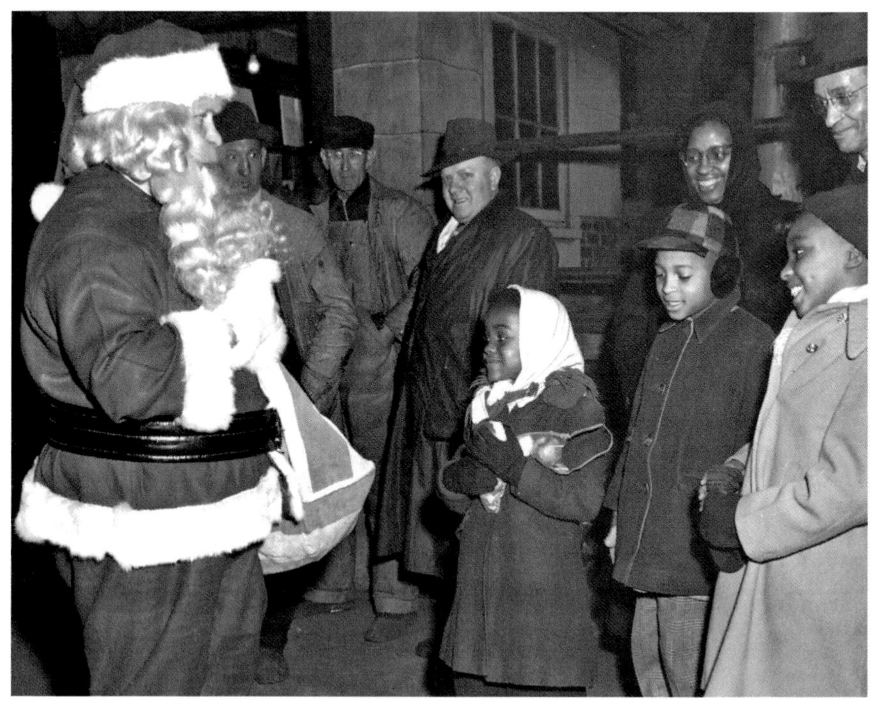

Greeters receive stockings from the N&W Santa along his holiday route at an on-line city stop, December 1950. *Courtesy Norfolk Southern Corp.*

Santa waves from the cab of N&W steam locomotive 1206, circa 1937. *Courtesy Norfolk Southern Corp.*

putting Santa aboard its trains. Old Saint Nick was provided with gifts to distribute and a schedule of every train the railroad operated in the days prior to Christmas. To our knowledge, he is the only Santa Claus to hand out red and green business cards, identifying himself as "Santa Claus—Representative—Norfolk & Western Railway."[123]

Santa traveled the N&W system by train from Cincinnati to Norfolk, up the Shenandoah Valley and down into North Carolina, handing out gift stockings to children and ladies and cigars to male passengers. Among the receipts kept on file at Norfolk Southern headquarters, in Norfolk, Virginia, are handwritten receipts for Santa's meals and lodging for the year 1950. N&W also paid the tab for Christmas music from Muzak to brighten the spirits on its trains, as well as the wages of its own Santa, Stuart Kelly.[124]

The N&W also worked closely with communities large and small to bring Santa to town. The *Norfolk & Western Magazine* (reprinted in the *Turntable Times*, a publication of the Roanoke Chapter of the National Railway Historical Society) records that on December 7, 1946, the Tennessean made an unscheduled stop at Vinton, Virginia, to drop off Santa. There, the mayor, other dignitaries, the William Byrd High School band and hundreds of citizens accompanied Santa as he boarded a red and white float for a parade. Two weeks later, when train Number 35 chugged into South Boston, Virginia, a crowd estimated at between three and five thousand was waiting, cheering so loud that Santa almost couldn't be heard.[125]

Santa also detrained at Crewe, Virginia, a town that owes its existence to the N&W, which today houses an unmatched collection of memorabilia that aided us in our research for this book.

Always proud of its service to patrons, the N&W even had Santa accompanied for a couple days by the company photographer, who captured some of the classic images of the way the railroad reached out to become part of the community. In each of those communities, it made a conscious pledge to serve, going back to the early days of America's railroads, when locomotives burned wood. The Norfolk, Virginia staff of the historical archives department of successor railroad Norfolk Southern has preserved those images and generously made them available for this publication—most certainly, an early Christmas present for us, its grateful authors.

CHAPTER 17

THE PARTY'S OVER

Even though the Cox Santa Claus Specials ended in Ashland after 1958, despite the inability of Norfolk & Western and Miller & Rhoads to reach an agreement that would have extended the life of the Roanoke and Lynchburg promotions beyond 1959, and the short life of the Petersburg Atlantic Coast Line specials that came and went between 1960 and 1963, Virginia's Santa Trains flourished for roughly a decade. They became a much-awaited part of the holiday season. The RF&P was operating upward of a dozen trains from Alexandria and Richmond annually, as well as one or two Fredericksburg moves each year. In 1962, according to a copy of *Rail-O-Gram*, RF&P's special trains carried 43,200 passengers, and the number of trains and riders grew steadily.[126]

Gene Luck was already fifty-one years old when he was hired by the RF&P in 1955. It's said that when you enjoy your job, it isn't work. While that might be true, in 1969, at age sixty-five, he announced his retirement. He wanted to travel on his own, with his wife, on their schedule and at their own leisure. Friendly and outgoing, Luck wished to take a more active role at First English Lutheran Church. He served as a director of the downtown Richmond YMCA, where he was regarded as a champion handball player, an activity he finally gave up at age seventy-eight. No doubt his participation in that strenuous sport attributed to his good health and long life. He died in 1993 at the age of eighty-eight.[127]

Sadly, he would outlive his young assistant and successor, William A. Griffin. In Billy, he had found someone who was just as enthusiastic as he had been. Luck was confident that RF&P's special train service would continue to thrive. While it did, the general downward trend of passenger train ridership accelerated nationally.

When the U.S. Postal Service announced that it would cancel lucrative contracts under which railroads hauled first-class mail, the Interstate Commerce Commission was immediately deluged with applications to discontinue most passenger trains. If granted, it would have meant the end of all rail passenger service with the possible exception of that which existed along the densely populated Northeast corridor.

A clamor arose in Congress for outright subsidies to continue passenger train service. Others suggested that the entire U.S. railroad industry should be federalized. A compromise was reached, and President Richard M. Nixon signed into law legislation creating the quasi-government National Railroad Passenger Corporation—Amtrak. When it assumed responsibility for almost all passenger train operations in the United States on May 1, 1971, Gene

Employees Gene Luck (left) and William A. Griffin pose at the start of another RF&P special train, January 1963. *William E. Griffin Private Collection.*

Luck's special trains program came to an end, as did all of the RF&P's passenger service. Most dearly missed would be the Santa Trains.

In exchange for its locomotives and passenger equipment, each railroad that agreed to join Amtrak would be relieved of operating any passenger trains except those designated by the U.S. Department of Transportation as part of the Amtrak original system. Only three trains (New York–Florida Silver Star, Silver Meteor and Champion) would operate over RF&P rails. Amtrak entered into contracts with the RF&P to operate only those trains and only under specified terms. Any additional trains Amtrak might ask to operate would have to be paid for at a cost determined by the railroad.

As such, with only a skeletal management staff and extremely limited resources, Amtrak initially declined requests to operate any extra trains—hence, no 1971 Santa Trains. After some behind-the-scenes negotiations, however, Amtrak was persuaded to accommodate Miller & Rhoads in Richmond only for one last Christmas season. Neither the Alexandria nor the Fredericksburg trains ran, however.

"I remember when Amtrak decided to end the Santa trips and how disappointed everyone was, especially the store executives," recalled Hank Coghill, who was the general manager at the downtown Richmond Miller & Rhoads store at the time. "I do recall that there were negotiations between M&R and Amtrak to let the Santa Trains run that last year."[128]

Newly hired Miller & Rhoads Snow Queen and coauthor Donna Strother Deekens filled in as the train's Snow Queen for at least one day during that final 1971 Richmond–Ashland Santa Train run.

While it is tempting to cite Amtrak for the discontinuance of the Santa Trains, they would have eventually disappeared nonetheless. In 1989, after a number of ownership changes, Miller & Rhoads went out of business. On October 10, 1991, the Richmond, Fredericksburg & Potomac Railroad Company, after 157 years of continuous operation, was acquired by CSX Transportation.

Communities wishing to have Santa arrive amid pomp and circumstance turned to various alternative modes of transportation. As Thalhimers department store in Richmond had done in 1939 with a gyrocopter, some towns dropped Saint Nick in by parachute or in a plane. In Portsmouth, Virginia, in 2012, he arrived with his Snow Queen, Donna Strother Deekens, on a fireboat. Santa began touring South Hill, Virginia, in a fire truck in the 2000s, as well. In 1979, the jolly ol' elf showed up on the steps of Thomas Jefferson's Virginia State Capitol Building in a 1913 Ford Model T, to greet then governor John N. Dalton.

Thalhimers department store advertisement announcing Santa's arrival by gyrocopter at Hermitage Air Field in Richmond, Virginia, 1939. *Lewis Parks Private Collection.*

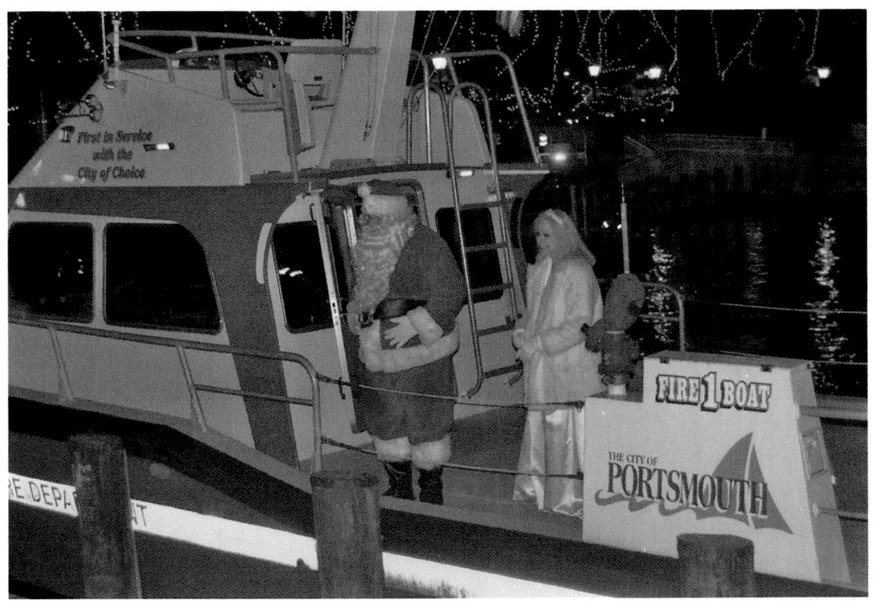

Santa and Snow Queen Donna Strother Deekens arrive by a City of Portsmouth fireboat, December 8, 2012. *Courtesy Clyde W. Nordan–Olde Towne Photos.*

Following years at Miller & Rhoads, Santa appeared in the South Hill, Virginia Christmas Parade, arriving on a fire truck, circa 2010. *Santa Charlie Private Collection.*

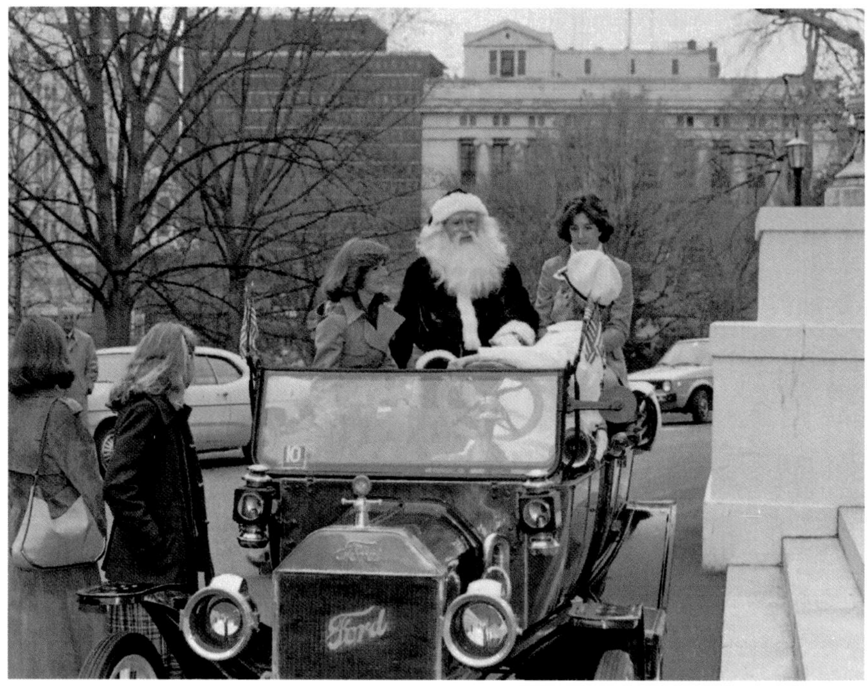

Miller & Rhoads' Santa arrives at Virginia's state capitol in 1979 in a 1913 Model T Ford, driven by Henry Gonner. *Hank Gonner Private Collection.*

Remembering the original 1955 Cox promotion, in 1983, the merchants in Ashland's Henry Clay Shopping Center harkened back to the past by arranging for Santa to arrive on a regularly scheduled Amtrak train. Just as in the days of Joe and Jacqueline Andrews, he was met by an enthusiastic crowd numbering into the hundreds. There, Santa boarded a fire truck for his ride to the shopping center on England Street.

Anxious to preserve yet another part of Richmond's railroad history, in conjunction with Robert Bryant, a railroad executive who leased a short C&O Railroad branch in Buckingham County, the Old Dominion Chapter of the National Railway Historical Society began to operate a series of passenger excursions. These included some short-distance December runs behind a vintage RF&P diesel-electric locomotive, obtained by the chapter, and a couple of coach cars that coincidentally were part of the original RF&P Santa Trains. With Santa aboard, the trains have generated quite a bit of tourism for the small town of Dillwyn, Virginia. Tickets are quickly sold out each season.

Santa Claus meets with an adoring crowd in Ashland, Virginia, during a holiday train stop, December 1982. *From* Herald-Progress *image, courtesy McGraw-Page Library, Randolph-Macon College.*

In 2004, local Ashland Train Town Toy & Hobby Shop owner Jim Donlan arranged for a Santa Train that was in fact Amtrak's regularly scheduled Twilight Shoreliner, Number 67, that stopped in Ashland before continuing on to the colonial capital of Williamsburg. There, the train's patrons boarded its northbound counterpart, Number 66, which returned them to Ashland. "Mr. and Mrs. Claus were aboard and it was always a sellout," Donlan proudly noted.[129]

Lamenting the loss of Alexandria's Santa Train, in 2008, Walter Loftin, the now-retired RF&P ticket agent, while visiting a local hobby shop, suggested a revival of Northern Virginia's Santa excursions. He proposed that the management of the Virginia Railway Express (VRE), a commuter service supported by a number of Northern Virginia transportation authorities, be approached about operating weekend Santa Trains with their normally idle equipment. While they were sympathetic, VRE simply did not have the resources to offer the service, and doing so would mean asking host railroads, CSX and Norfolk Southern, to permit additional operation over their tracks.

Some original RF&P equipment continues Santa Trains from Dillwyn, Virginia. This one was sponsored by Old Dominion Chapter, NRHS, December 4, 2010. *Bob Dickinson Private Collection.*

Not to be deterred, the group asked if there would be a prohibition from selling round-trip tickets from Alexandria to Manassas on a scheduled train, on which Santa and Mrs. Claus could ride and greet escorted children during the hour-long layover in Manassas. VRE agreed to allow what is now called the Santa Express, which is always a sellout.

After obtaining permission from CSX Transportation a couple years later, VRE began scheduling Santa Trains on its Fredericksburg line on weekends. James "Chipp" Boone Jr., of Keolis Rail Services Virginia, the current operator of both Manassas and Fredericksburg VRE lines, personally oversees the eagerly anticipated trains that are named to honor some of Santa's reindeer.

The VRE's relatively new double-decked equipment is not the same as the comfortable, old, surplus RF&P 500-series cars of the very first Santa

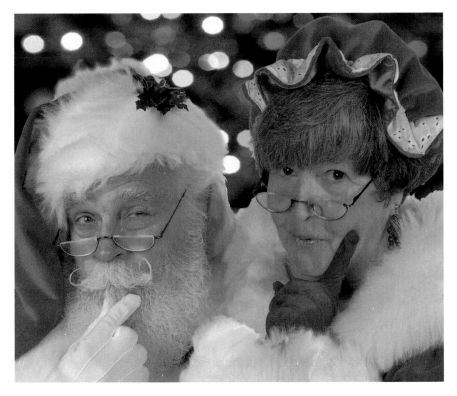

Santa and Mrs. Claus are a fixture on the Virginia Railway Express (VRE) "Santa Express," December 2012. *Santa Jack Private Collection.*

Packed with Fredericksburg, Virginia youngsters, VRE Santa Train "Dasher" crosses the Rappahannock River traveling toward the North Pole on December 10, 2011. *Bill Whitbeck Private Collection.*

VRE conductor observes as Santa and Mrs. Claus pose at Woodbridge, Virginia, December 2012. *James "Chipp" Boone Jr. Private Collection, Keolis Rail Service Virginia, VRE.*

Claus Trains. VRE passengers sit on bright, colorful seats with digital information displays and electronic intercom systems. There are no big thick red cushions on which you can jump up and down and watch the dust fly, as we did when we boarded the Miller & Rhoads Santa Train at Broad Street Station. The station, in fact, is now a science museum, whose biggest attraction is the annual model train show. Other than that, no trains of any kind call there. And even though you can still hop aboard a couple of the original heavyweight RF&P coach cars for the Buckingham Branch Santa Train at Dillwyn, it might not seem the same, but then, nothing stays the same. Someday, however, the children who ride today's Santa Trains will no doubt look back nostalgically at their experiences, just as we are able to do.

It's been nearly twenty-five years since the Lionel Super Chief skirted along the edge of the huge corner display window at Miller & Rhoads, but for Joe Pace of Wilmington, North Carolina, the memories will always be there: "I think my parents used to tip the doorman at the Hotel John Marshall to keep an eye on me and my brother when we'd slip out the door to spend hours watching [the trains] when we came to Richmond on shopping trips."[130] And George Thomas Parsons III, now living in Texas, still recalls

The Santa Train halts at Dillwyn, Virginia, for Santa to climb aboard, sponsored by Old Dominion Chapter, NRHS, December 5, 2009. *Bob Dickinson Private Collection.*

The Miller & Rhoads Richmond train display windows proved very popular because they featured scale models of local landmarks and Miller & Rhoads stores. *Milton Burke Private Collection.*

Miller & Rhoads Santa holds sleeping children, fatigued following the Santa Train ride, circa 1962. *Paul Mitchell, Tim Mitchell and Mary Mitchell Amos Private Collection.*

his grandmother saying, "You'd reach through that window and play with those trains if you could."[131]

"Trains, Santa and Christmas all seem to go together, just like in *The Polar Express*," Celeste Heath of Alexandria recalled in a letter to us. "Those memories still make Christmas magical today."[132] Tina Currie of Mechanicsville, who rode the train with sister Nancy Bumgardner and their cousins, fondly recalled, "I even took my oldest child on the trip before it was discontinued. I would really love to see this revived so I could take my grandchildren." Three generations of experience on the Santa Trains, if you can imagine.[133]

To the children who ride today, though, like their parents and grandparents from nearly sixty years ago, what they will be able to share with their own children and grandchildren will be the joy of Christmas music, the taste of candy canes, the sound of laughing clowns and the giggles of smiling elves. The recollections forever etched in their youthful minds will be of the time when they were aboard that special train, when Santa Claus came into town—on a rail.

NOTES

Introduction

1. Valentine Davies, *Miracle on 34th Street*, DVD, directed by George Seaton (New York: Twentieth Century Fox, 1947).
2. Donna Strother Deekens, *Christmas at Miller & Rhoads: Memoirs of a Snow Queen* (Charleston, SC: The History Press, 2009), 28.

Chapter 1

3. Carlton Norris McKenney, *Rails in Richmond* (Glendale, CA: Interurban Press, 1986), 25.
4. Interview with Bob Luck, June 10, 2013.
5. Ibid.

Chapter 2

6. Telephone interview with Jerry Maxey, March 20, 2013.
7. Interview with Betty Carol Stevenson, August 3, 2013.
8. Ibid., April 9, 2013.
9. Ibid.
10. Interview with Tom Wulf, April 18, 2013.
11. Telephone interview with Sumpter Priddy Jr., April 30, 2013.
12. Interview with Cecile Andrews Cox, April 25, 2013.

13. Deekens, *Christmas*, 26.
14. Telephone interview with Gwen Jeffers Downey, June 5, 2013.
15. Ashland Sesquicentennial Committee, *Ashland, Virginia: 150 Years 1858–2008* (Rich Hill, MO: Bell Books, 2009), 140.
16. Telephone interview with Gwen Jeffers Downey, June 5, 2013.
17. *Herald-Progress*, November 17, 1955.
18. Ibid., December 1, 1955.

Chapter 3

19. William E. Griffin Jr., *150 Years of History: Along the Richmond, Fredericksburg and Potomac Railroad* (Richmond, VA: Whittet & Shepperson, 1984), 39.

Chapter 4

20. *Naked City*, Screen Gems Television, Culver City, CA, 1958–1963.
21. Griffin, *150 Years of History*, 39.

Chapter 5

22. Telephone interview with Sarah Wright, June 6, 2013.

Chapter 6

23. Telephone interview with Hazel Moore, April 12, 2013.
24. *Herald-Progress*, November 21, 1957.
25. Interview with Cecile Andrews Cox, April 25, 2013.
26. Ibid.
27. Interview with Betty Carol Stevenson, April 9, 2013.
28. *Herald-Progress*, December 5, 1957.
29. Interview with Betty Carol Stevenson, April 9, 2013.
30. *Herald-Progress*, December 12, 1957.
31. Ibid.
32. Interview with Betty Carol Stevenson, April 9, 2013.
33. Telephone interview with Sumpter Priddy Jr., April 30, 2013.

34. Interview with Betty Carol Stevenson, April 9, 2013.
35. *Herald-Progress*, December 12, 1957.

Chapter 7

36. Telephone interview with Paul Pearce, April 4, 2013.
37. Telephone interview with Fred Dill, July 7, 2013.
38. Marilyn Hood Gunn to the authors, July 12, 2013.
39. Earle Dunford and George Bryson, *Under the Clock: The Story of Miller & Rhoads* (Charleston, SC: The History Press, 2008), 93–96.

Chapter 8

40. Interview with Bob Luck, June 10, 2013.

Chapter 9

41. Telephone interview with Bobbie Kay Wash, April 22, 2013.
42. Nancy Allen Perrow to the authors, June 9, 2013.
43. Telephone interview with Ed Crews, April 22, 2013.
44. Interview with Calvin Boles, May 30, 2013.
45. Nancy Bendall Emerson to the authors, February 5, 2013.
46. Telephone interview with John Strother, March 26, 2013.
47. Telephone interview with Graham Wilson, April 7, 2013.
48. Interview with Dan Rowe, July 15, 2013.
49. Interview with Carol Bryson, June 7, 2013.
50. Interview with Sue Ferrell, June 7, 2013.
51. Telephone interview with Ed Crews, April 22, 2013.
52. Perrow to the authors, June 9, 2013.
53. Charles Curley III to the authors, April 8, 2013.
54. William Barnett to the authors, April 11, 2013.
55. *The Highland Fling* 18, no. 2, Highland Spring High School, Highland Springs, VA, September 24, 1965.
56. Telephone interview with Ed Crews, April 22, 2013.
57. Telephone interview with Judith Valentine Frayser, June 19, 2013.
58. Interview with Cheryl Wakefield Hamm, April 2, 2013.
59. Telephone interview with Jean Howe Duke, April 24, 2013.

60. Interview with Dan Rowe, July 15, 2013.
61. Arthur "Chuck" Hood in a general letter, addressing "What Was the Best Christmas Present I Ever Received?" circa 1970s.
62. Interview with Charles Nuckols, April 30, 2013.
63. Perrow to authors, June 9, 2013.

Chapter 10

64. Richmond, Fredericksburg & Potomac Railroad, Annual Report, 1957.
65. Interview with Kenneth Miller, April 20, 2013.
66. Griffin, *150 Years of History*, 39.
67. Interview with Bill Deekens, August 6, 2013.
68. Interview with Bob Luck, June 10, 2013.

Chapter 11

69. Interview with Claudine Miller, April 20, 2013.
70. Telephone interview with Julia Stewart Milton, April 12, 2013.
71. Interview with George Bryson, June 7, 2013.
72. Interview with Kenneth Miller, April 20, 2013.
73. Telephone interview with Ginger Hibbetts Sweet, June 22, 2013.
74. Ibid.
75. William E. Warden, revised by Kenneth Miller, *Norfolk & Western Passenger Service, 1946–1971* (Lynchburg, VA: TLC Publishing, Inc., 2000), iii.
76. Telephone interview with Ginger Hibbetts Sweet, June 22, 2013.
77. Telephone interview with Julia Stewart Milton, April 12, 2013.
78. Ibid.
79. Interview with Claudine Miller, April 20, 2013.
80. *Rail-O-Gram*, RF&P employee newsletter (January 1959), 3.
81. Interview with George Bryson, June 7, 2013.

Chapter 12

82. *N&W Railway Magazine* (January 1960): 17.
83. Telephone interview with Lee Hawkins, August 6, 2013.
84. Ibid.
85. *N&W Railway Magazine* (January 1960): 17.

86. Interview with George Bryson, June 7, 2013.
87. Interview with Claudine Miller, April 20, 2013.

Chapter 13

88. *Rail-O-Gram* (January 1959): 2.
89. Interview with George Bryson, June 7, 2013.
90. Telephone interview with Walter Loftin, June 24, 2013.
91. Telephone interview with Jacqueline Stewart, June 6, 2013.
92. *Rail-O-Gram* (January 1967).
93. Telephone interview with Dale Latham, June 6, 2013.
94. *Rail-O-Gram* (January 1967).
95. *Highball*, Old Dominion Chapter, National Railway Historical Society (January 1965).
96. *Progress-Index (Petersburg, VA)*, December 11, 1960, 1.
97. American Legion Post #136, Ettrick, VA.
98. Telephone interview with Annabel Woodriff Newton, July 11, 2013.
99. Telephone interview with Edythe Gill, July 16, 2013
100. Ibid.
101. Telephone interview with Annabel Woodriff Newton, July 11, 2013.

Chapter 14

102. Dunford and Bryson, *Under the Clock*, 93.
103. Telephone interview with Bill Schafer, May 14, 2013.
104. Telephone interview with Walter Loftin, June 24, 2013.
105. Interview with John W. West III, May 28, 2013.
106. Telephone interview with Nancy Pace Newton, April 24, 2013.
107. *Highball*, ODC, NRHS, September, 1966.
108. Telephone interview with Lee Milstead, June 26, 2013.

Chapter 15

109. Interview with Nancy Cogsdale, June 13, 2013.
110. H. Reid, *Extra South* (Susquehanna, PA: Starruuca Valley Publications, 1964), 28–9.
111. *Sedley Theatre Movie Guide*, December 10, 1950.

112. Telephone interview with Patricia Duck Carter, June 18, 2013.
113. Interview with Nancy Cogsdale, June 13, 2013; telephone interview with Patricia Duck Carter, June 18, 2013.
114. Interview with Nancy Cogsdale, June 13, 2013.
115. Telephone interview with Joan Hundley Powell, June 13, 2013.
116. Telephone interview with Patricia Duck Carter, June 18, 2013.
117. Telephone interview with Wesley Wills, July 17, 2013.
118. Telephone interview with Donna Neal Turner, June 9, 2013.
119. Telephone interview with June Hundley Dunlow, June 10, 2013; "Nostalgia Trip," Mary D. Hundley, 1986.
120. Telephone interview with Joe Brinkley Jr., June 24, 2013.

Chapter 16

121. Interview with Jim Grem, June 17, 2013.
122. Henry C. Walsh, *Santa Claus on the Train*, 1863–1927.
123. Norfolk Southern Corp., May 16, 2013.
124. Ibid.
125. *Turntable Times* 38, no. 7 (November/December 2006), Roanoke Chapter, National Railway Historical Society.

Chapter 17

126. *Rail-O-Gram* (January 1963).
127. Telephone interview with Bob Luck, June 10, 2013.
128. Telephone interview with Hank Coghill, April 17, 2013.
129. Telephone interview with Jim Donlan, February 4, 2013.
130. Joe Pace to the authors, February 5, 2013.
131. George Thomas Parsons III to the authors, May 7, 2013.
132. Celeste Heath to the authors, July 11, 2013.
133. Interview with Tina Currie and Nancy Bumgardner, July 20, 2013.

ABOUT THE AUTHORS

Donna Strother Deekens

Donna Strother Deekens is owner and party director of a traveling tea party business, Teapots, Treats & Traditions. A graduate of Westhampton College of the University of Richmond, she has performed professionally as an actress, soloist, entertainer and public speaker. She enjoyed playing the role of a Snow Queen for many years at the Miller & Rhoads downtown Richmond department store and was privileged to ride on the Santa Train from Richmond to Ashland in 1971 as Snow Queen. In addition to her entertainment background, she has held positions in public relations, marketing and fundraising for government, corporate and nonprofit organizations. She is the author of two books, *Christmas at Miller & Rhoads: Memoirs of a Snow Queen* and *Santaland: A Miller & Rhoads Christmas*. She is married to Bill Deekens, and they have two sons, Brent and Greg, as well as a devoted dog, Missy.

Donna Strother Deekens. *Courtesy Clyde W. Nordan–Olde Towne Photos.*

Doug Riddell

Doug Riddell. *Courtesy Doug Riddell.*

Readers worldwide know retired Amtrak locomotive engineer, company photographer, author and magazine columnist Doug Riddell from over twenty years of anecdotal insight into life on the railroad. His first book, *From the Cab: Stories from a Locomotive Engineer*, was published in 1999. The Richmond, Virginia native, broadcaster, journalist and pubic speaker earned his bachelor's degree in mass communications from Virginia Commonwealth University. Quite appropriately, freight and passenger trains endlessly rumble down the middle of Railroad Avenue, past the quaint shops and large antebellum homes of picturesque Ashland, Virginia, where Doug lives with his wife, Sandy. Their son, Ryan, is an Amtrak locomotive engineer.